BTEC
Apprenticeships

2
Level

HEALTH & SOCIAL CARE
Assessment Workbook

LEISA ANDERTON, BRENDA BAKER & CARON KEYS

www.btecapprenticeships.com

AYS LEARNING

PEARSON

Published by Pearson Education Limited, a company incorporated in England and Wales, having its registered office at Edinburgh Gate, Harlow, Essex, CM20 2JE. Registered company number: 872828

www.pearsonschoolsandfecolleges.co.uk

Text © Pearson Education Ltd 2011
Designed by AM Design
Typeset by Tek-Art
Original illustrations © Pearson Education 2011
Illustrated by Tek-Art and Vicky Woodgate
Original cover design by Wooden Ark
Picture research by Susie Prescott
Cover photo/illustration © Corbis: Patrick Sheandell O'Carroll/PhotoAlto

The rights of Caron Keys, Leisa Anderton and Brenda Baker to be identified as authors of this work have been asserted by them in accordance with the Copyright, Designs and Patents Act 1988.

First published 2011

15 14 13 12 11
10 9 8 7 6 5 4 3 2 1

British Library Cataloguing in Publication Data
A catalogue record for this book is available from the British Library

ISBN 978 1 446900 34 5

Printed in the UK by Ashford Colour Press Ltd.

Acknowledgements
The publisher would like to thank the following for their kind permission to reproduce their photographs:

(Key: b-bottom; c-centre; l-left; r-right; t-top)

Alamy Images: BrazilPhotos.com 46, Corbis Bridge 65, Fancy 6, Paula Solloway 55; Getty Images: Joselito Briones / The Image Bank 49; Pearson Education Ltd: Gareth Boden 60, Jules Selmes 23, 26, 31, Lord and Leverett 37, 40, Steve Shott 19; Photolibrary.com: Jacky Chapman 1; Shutterstock.com: Alexander Raths 39, 68bl/7, Anita Patterson 68cr/4, barbaradudzinska 68cl/3, Dean Mitchell 45, Gillmar 68tr/2, Isantill 68l/5, Jiri Hera 68tl/1, Magone 68br/8, Naturaldigital 68r/6

All other images © Pearson Education

Every effort has been made to contact copyright holders of material reproduced in this book. Any omissions will be rectified in subsequent printings if notice is given to the publishers.

Pearson Education Limited is not responsible for the content of any external internet sites. It is essential for tutors to preview each website before using it in class so as to ensure that the URL is still accurate, relevant and appropriate. We suggest that tutors bookmark useful websites and consider enabling students to access them through the school/college intranet.

Disclaimer
This material has been published on behalf of Edexcel and offers high-quality support for the delivery of Edexcel qualifications. This does not mean that the material is essential to achieve any Edexcel qualification, nor does it mean that it is the only suitable material available to support any Edexcel qualification. Material from this publication will not be used verbatim in any examination or assessment set by Edexcel. Any resource lists produced by Edexcel shall include this and other appropriate resources.

Copies of official specifications for all Edexcel qualifications may be found on the Edexcel website: www.edexcel.com

> Additional support for using this Assessment Workbook is available from
> www.btecapprenticeshipworkbooks.co.uk
>
> **Username:** hsc2
> **Password:** hsc2learn

BTEC APPRENTICESHIP LEVEL 2 HEALTH AND SOCIAL CARE

Apprentice name	
Apprentice number	
Assessor's name	
Training provider	
Employer	

The candidate has successfully completed all relevant sections of the BTEC Apprenticeship Assessment Workbook	
Assessor's signature:	Date:
I confirm that all the work submitted is my own and that all sources of information have been fully acknowledged	
Apprentice's signature:	Date:

There is a glossary on page xiv explaining key terms that you will come across frequently during your Apprenticeship. These words appear in **bold** when they first come up in this introduction.

INTRODUCTION TO YOUR BTEC APPRENTICESHIP

An Apprenticeship is a work-based qualification. While you are working for your employer and developing your skills and knowledge in the workplace, you will also have regular contact with an **assessor**. Your assessor will support you in your learning and assessment, possibly sometimes at a local college or training centre.

Your Level 2 Intermediate BTEC Apprenticeship in Health and Social Care may consist of the following qualifications:

- Diploma Level 2 Health and Social Care

- BTEC Level 2 Certificate in Preparing to Work in Adult Social Care

- BTEC WorkSkills for Effective Learning and Employment

- Functional Skills at Level 1 in English and Mathematics

- OR Key Skills at Level 1 in Communication and Application of Number (only until September 2012)

- OR Essential Skills Wales at Level 1 in Communication and Application of Number (if you are based in Wales)

- Employment Responsibilities and Rights in Health, Social Care, Children and Young People's Settings

- Personal, Learning and Thinking Skills (in England only).

All of these qualifications, apart from Functional Skills and part of Key Skills, can be assessed through practical work-based activities, evidence of what you do in your day-to-day job, and discussions and observations with your assessor.

ASSESSMENT

This Assessment Workbook will help you make the most of the different assessment options that are available for your Apprenticeship. You may be assessed through:

- work tasks that let you demonstrate your **competence**

- observations of you completing work tasks

- discussions with your assessor that demonstrate your knowledge and understanding

- written **evidence**, for example completed Knowledge and Understanding pages from this Assessment Workbook.

Any assessment work will need to be recorded for your **portfolio**. Your assessor will advise you of the best methods of recording this evidence. Because you may work with confidential information, your portfolio should contain the location of any naturally occurring workplace evidence (such as letters or reports) rather than a copy of the documents themselves.

Your assessor will let you know if the BTEC Certificate will be assessed using onscreen tests. If you are being assessed onscreen, you may find the interactive quizzes provided at www.btecapprenticeshipworkbooks.co.uk help prepare you for the test.

Your assessor will help you select the units of the different qualifications that best suit your needs and the needs of your employer. This Assessment Workbook does not cover every optional unit in the qualification, so your assessor will let you know which sections of the Assessment Workbook are most relevant for your Apprenticeship.

As part of your Apprenticeship, you may need to pass the Functional Skills qualifications listed above. These are assessed through timed tests, which may be paper-based or onscreen. Your assessor will advise you of when you will sit these and will help you prepare for the assessment. You can find practice assessment activities at www.btecapprenticeshipworkbooks.co.uk. If you are taking Key Skills or Essential Skills Wales instead, your assessor will discuss with you when and how you will complete this assessment.

THE ROLE OF YOUR EMPLOYER

During your BTEC Apprenticeship, your employer needs to provide you with:

- enough time to allow you to complete your Apprenticeship work
- opportunities to demonstrate the necessary skills in your workplace
- a mentor to help provide informal training and support
- a wage.

In addition, your employer (or your colleagues) may support you in completing your Apprenticeship through:

- providing **witness statements** that can be used as evidence for your Apprenticeship
- additional training where you need to develop your skills and knowledge further
- support and guidance if you have any human resources issues.

THE ROLE OF YOUR ASSESSOR

Your assessor will support you in completing your BTEC Apprenticeship. They will visit you at your workplace and discuss the Apprenticeship with you to make sure the qualifications are suitable for your needs and job role, and that you fully understand what you will need to learn and do during the Apprenticeship programme.

v

During your Apprenticeship, your assessor needs to:

- make sure you understand how you will be assessed and what you will be assessed on

- give you good notice of each time they visit you at your workplace, and what you need to have completed in preparation for the visit

- discuss your work and your job role with your employer and colleagues to gather additional evidence for your portfolio.

In addition, your assessor may recommend supporting resources, such as textbooks or e-learning, that you need to use during the course of the Apprenticeship to help you build your knowledge and skills.

YOUR ROLE

You are responsible for both carrying out the job that your employer is paying you to do and for completing your Apprenticeship. Your responsibilities to your employer are:

- to do the work required of you to a satisfactory standard

- to keep your employer informed of how you are progressing through the Apprenticeship

- to meet the general requirements of an employee at your workplace (for example, to turn up on time).

You also have responsibilities to your assessor. Your assessor will need you to:

- inform your employer of the dates when your assessor is visiting you at your workplace

- complete the work required of you by the date agreed, and if you are unable to do so, keep your assessor informed of your progress

- attend any training organised by your **training provider**

- keep them informed of the work activities you are planning to carry out on the dates of your assessor visits – if you will not be in the workplace on that day, tell your assessor as soon as possible so they can reschedule the visit

- make sure your work is your own and that you indicate the original source of any information or wording that you have found somewhere else (for example, on the Internet).

HOW TO USE THIS BTEC APPRENTICESHIP ASSESSMENT WORKBOOK

This BTEC Apprenticeship Assessment Workbook has been designed to support you and your assessor in completing your BTEC Apprenticeship. It helps you to prove your knowledge, understanding and skills, and identify evidence that will demonstrate your competence and go towards achieving your Apprenticeship.

As you will be submitting this Assessment Workbook to your assessor as evidence for your Apprenticeship, you need to make sure you keep it safe and update it regularly.

WHAT THE ASSESSMENT WORKBOOK COVERS

Your assessor will discuss your Apprenticeship with you and will identify a number of units that will be relevant to you and your job role. This Assessment Workbook covers the mandatory units and a selection of optional units to complete the qualifications that make up the BTEC Apprenticeship.

	Credits	Mandatory / Optional
BTEC Level 2 Certificate in Preparing to Work in Adult Social Care		
Unit 1 Principles of communication in adult social care settings	2	M
Unit 2 Principles of personal development in adult social care settings	2	M
Unit 3 Principles of diversity, equality and inclusion in adult social care settings	2	M
Unit 4 Principles of safeguarding and protection in health and social care	3	M
Unit 5 Introduction to duty of care in health, social care or children's and young people's settings	1	M
Unit 6 Understand the role of the social care worker	1	M
Unit 7 Understand person-centred approaches in adult social care settings	4	M
Unit 8 Understand health and safety in social care settings	4	M
Unit 9 Understand how to handle information in social care	1	M
Diploma Level 2 Health and Social Care		
Unit 1 (SHC 21) Introduction to communication in health, social care or children's and young people's settings	3	M
Unit 2 (SHC 22) Introduction to personal development in health, social care or children's and young people's settings	3	M
Unit 3 (SHC 23) Introduction to equality and inclusion in health, social care or children's and young people's settings	2	M

Unit 4	(SHC 24) Introduction to duty of care in health, social care or children's and young people's settings	1	M
Unit 5	(HSC 024) Principles of safeguarding and protection in health and social care	3	M
Unit 6	(HSC 025) The role of the health and social care worker	2	M
Unit 7	(HSC 026) Implement person-centred approaches in health and social care	5	M
Unit 8	(HSC 027) Contribute to health and safety in health and social care	4	M
Unit 9	(HSC 028) Handle information in health and social care settings	1	M
Unit 34	(SS MU 2.1) Introductory awareness of sensory loss	2	O
Unit 46	(HSC2002) Provide support for mobility	2	O
Unit 51	(HSC2007) Support independence in the tasks of daily living	5	O
Unit 55	(HSC2012) Support individuals who are distressed	3	O
Unit 56	(HSC2013) Support care plan activities	2	O
Unit 57	(HSC2014) Support individuals to eat and drink	2	O
Unit 58	(HSC2015) Support individuals to meet personal care needs	2	O
Unit 68	(HSC2028) Move and position individuals in accordance with their plan of care	4	O
Level 2 WorkSkills for Effective Learning and Employment			
Unit 1	Preparing for a level 2 Apprenticeship	1	M
Unit 3	Understanding employment responsibilities and rights in health, social care, children's and young people's settings	3	O
Unit 7	Using research skills to solve problems (CT/IE)	1	O
Unit 8	Participating through team leading (EP/TW)	1	O
Unit 9	Managing own learning (RL/SM)	1	O
Level 2	Award in employment responsibilities and rights in health, social care, children's and young people's settings	3	M

The Assessment Workbook also covers the Employment Rights and Responsibilities (ERR) and Personal, Learning and Thinking Skills (PLTS) requirements set by Skills for Care and Development for an Apprenticeship in Health and Social Care. This Assessment Workbook includes a section covering Employment Responsibilities and Rights in Health, Social Care, Children's and Young People's Settings.

Your assessor also has separate information showing how you can prove your basic skills if you are taking either Key Skills or Essential Skills Wales qualifications.

USING THE BTEC ASSESSMENT WORKBOOK

The Assessment Workbook contains a mixture of activities and guidance, which combine assessment criteria from these different qualifications and involve real work activities related to your day-to-day job. Your assessor will suggest which activities and sections you should complete and read at each point of your Apprenticeship. Use the activities and guidance to create or collect evidence, and to prepare for observations and professional discussions when your assessor visits you in your workplace.

In the margins of the Assessment Workbook you will see references to the assessment criteria covered by each activity. The following abbreviations have been used:

- Diploma = Level 2 Diploma

- BTEC = BTEC Level 2 Certificate

- WorkSkills = WorkSkills for Effective Learning and Employment

- PLTS = Personal, Learning and Thinking Skills.

The different activities and information in the Assessment Workbook are as follows.

KNOWLEDGE AND UNDERSTANDING TASKS

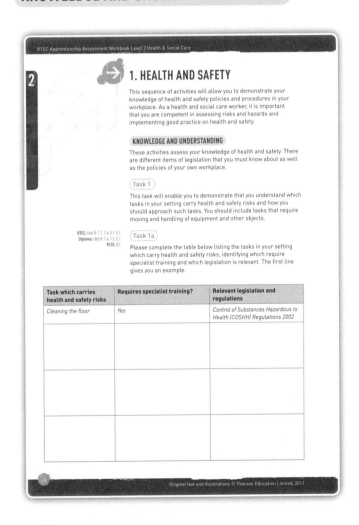

Complete these tasks to produce evidence of your knowledge and understanding of the different parts of your Apprenticeship. This may involve talking to your colleagues or manager, and will normally be completed before your assessor visits you in your workplace. Before each assessor visit, your assessor will discuss with you which activities they want you to complete.

You will also find electronic versions of these tasks online at www.btecapprenticeshipworkbooks.co.uk ready for you to type into and save. Your assessor will discuss with you how to complete the tasks.

EVIDENCE GATHERING

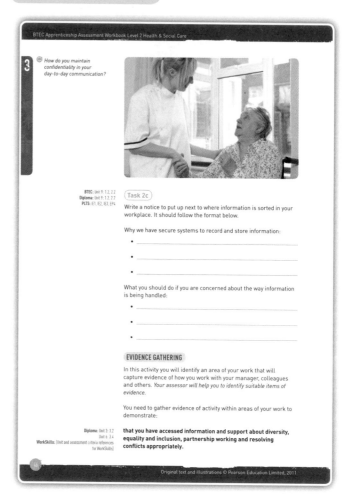

Use this information to identify where what you do in your everyday work can form part of the evidence you can submit for your Apprenticeship. This evidence needs to fit certain requirements, which are listed here, so make sure you check your evidence against these before including it in your portfolio.

PUTTING IT INTO PRACTICE

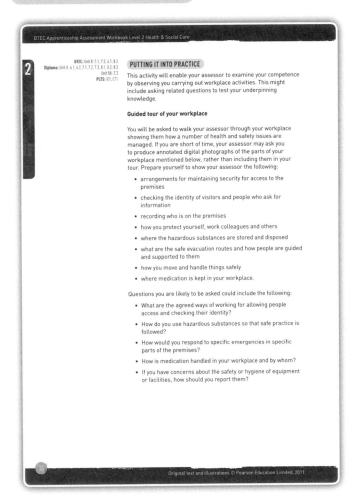

These sections prepare you for **observations**, when your assessor may want to observe you at work during their visits. Your assessor may also ask you questions about what you are doing to check your understanding, so make sure you read through the preparation notes provided here. They will discuss with you which of these sections you should read, depending on which work activities you are going to be carrying out when they next visit you at your workplace.

PROFESSIONAL DISCUSSION

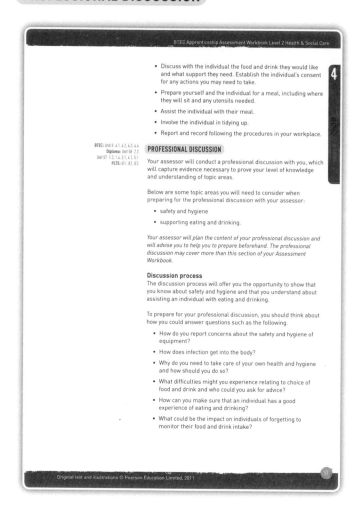

Your assessor will carry out, and record, **professional discussions** with you to check your knowledge, understanding and skills. They may combine the professional discussions from more than one section of the Assessment Workbook if they want to discuss several topics at the same time. These sections will help you prepare for discussion when your assessor visits you at your workplace.

www.btecapprenticeshipworkbooks.co.uk

There is a website that accompanies this Assessment Workbook, which contains the following additional support for you:

- Interactive revision activities to help you prepare for onscreen assessment for the BTEC Level 3 Certificate. (Your assessor will discuss and agree with you if you are going to use this kind of assessment.) You can, of course, also use these revision quizzes to check your knowledge if you are not using onscreen assessment.

- Electronic copies of the Knowledge and Understanding tasks from the Assessment Workbook that you can complete and save. You may need the latest version of Adobe Acrobat Reader to use these. The free software can be downloaded from http://get.adobe.com/reader/

- Practice Functional Skills activities to help you develop your skills and prepare you for the test.

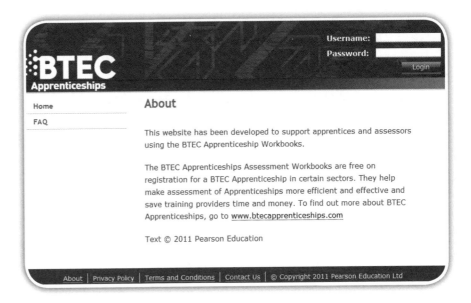

To log on to this website:

1   Go to www.btecapprenticeshipworkbooks.co.uk

2   In the login box on the top-right corner of your screen, use the following login details:
    Username: hsc2
    Password: hsc2learn

3   Click on 'Login'. You will then be able to select the support materials you want to use.

GLOSSARY

Below is a list of key terms that you will come across frequently in your Apprenticeship and the BTEC Apprenticeship Assessment Workbook.

Assessment criteria statements within a unit of a qualification describing the standards by which your skills or knowledge will be measured.

Assessor the person from your training provider who will visit you in your workplace; their role is to support you through your Apprenticeship and to assess your performance and knowledge.

Competence your skills and abilities in performing your work; competence means having the necessary knowledge and skills for your role.

Evidence anything that demonstrates you have the knowledge, understanding and skills specified in the assessment criteria.

Learning outcome statements within a unit of a qualification describing what you will have learned or be able to do once you have completed part of a unit.

Observation your assessor will watch you carrying out practical activities and parts of your job in order to judge your competence and will then keep a formal record of your performance.

Portfolio you and your assessor will need to record and organise the items of evidence you gather during your apprenticeship; a portfolio helps you to keep everything together and allows you to monitor your progress over time. Some training providers use paper-based portfolios, while others use e-portfolios, in which your evidence is recorded and stored digitally.

Professional discussion a structured conversation with your assessor which allows you to demonstrate your understanding of work practice or procedures and may also enable you to provide evidence of knowledge or competence.

Training provider a college or private training organisation responsible for assessing your competence in your workplace and, where necessary, for delivering additional training to develop your knowledge and skills.

Witness statement a statement which can support your evidence of competence, from a person who is qualified to make comments about your performance (for example, your manager). It must include: a description of the activity you have carried out; how it relates to the assessment criteria; when and in what context the activity was carried out.

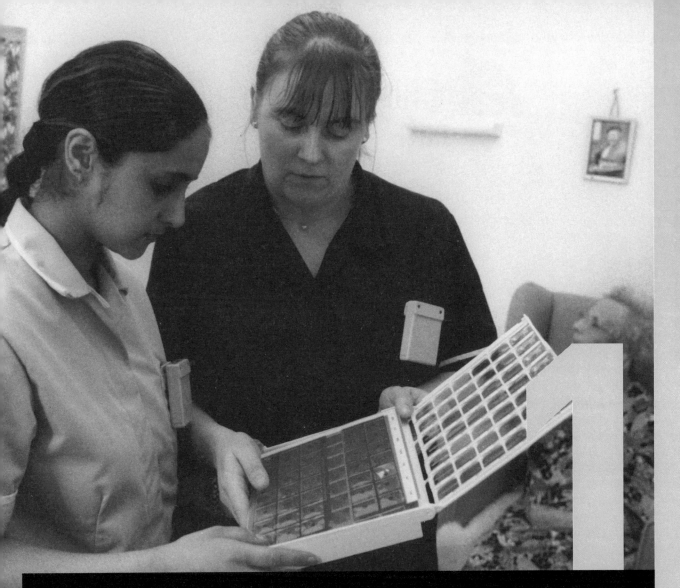

This induction section will enable you to show that you understand what the Apprenticeship Framework is and how it applies to you. You will show that you know about the sector you work in, about different career opportunities and that you have thought about your own strengths and weaknesses. You will show that you are able to follow the work practices that apply to your role.

In this section you will find a range of activities to help you prepare and gather evidence for your assessment related to the following topic:

→ 1. The Apprenticeship and your role

Before your assessor visits to check that you have completed this section of the Assessment Workbook, you will need to have drawn up your own development plan and be ready to show it to your assessor.

1. THE APPRENTICESHIP AND YOUR ROLE

In this induction section you will show that you understand the employer/employee relationship and what someone who works in the health and social care sector is required to do. The Workbook will help you to show that you follow agreed ways of working.

KNOWLEDGE AND UNDERSTANDING

WorkSkills: Unit 1: 1.1, 1.2

(Task 1)

(Task 1a)

Complete the spider diagram below to show that you understand what each component of the Apprenticeship is for and how it is assessed.

- In each box, for Number 1 say what the component is for.

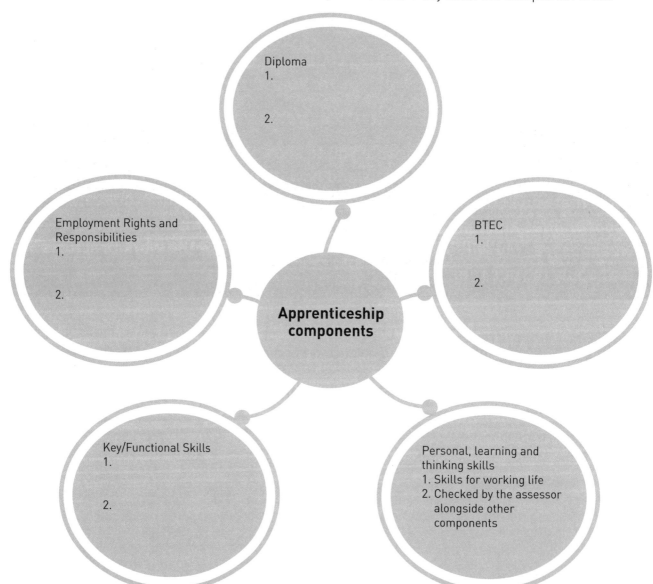

Diploma
1.

2.

Employment Rights and Responsibilities
1.

2.

BTEC
1.

2.

Apprenticeship components

Key/Functional Skills
1.

2.

Personal, learning and thinking skills
1. Skills for working life
2. Checked by the assessor alongside other components

1

- For Number 2 say how it is assessed. Types of assessment are given in a list below. Choose the most appropriate one or two.

Assessment methods:

- portfolio
- online test
- paper-based test.

One example has been done for you.

WorkSkills: Unit 1: 3.1, 3.2
ERR/WorkSkills: Unit 3: 4.1, 4.2, 4.3

Task 1b

In the table below write a list of different careers that you could aim to have after your Apprenticeship. In the second column, write in where you could get advice about how to progress on this career pathway. In the third column put two possible routes for this career path. An example has been done for you.

Career	Where to find advice	Progression routes
Nurse	*NHS careers advice website (www.nhscareers.nhs.uk/nursing.shtml)* *Union website (www.unison.org.uk/healthcare/nursing/education)*	*1. Level 3 BTEC* *2. University*
		1. 2.
		1. 2.
		1. 2.

1

BTEC: Unit 6:1.1
Diploma: Unit 6:1.1

(Task 2)

(Task 2a)

For each of the figures below, fill in the box for who you have personal or working relationships with and the box on why. An example has been completed for you.

Personal relationship

Who?

Family
_____
_____
_____
_____
_____

Why?

Love
_____
_____
_____
_____
_____

Working relationship

Who?

_____
_____
_____
_____
_____
_____

Why?

_____
_____
_____
_____
_____
_____

BTEC: Unit 6: 1.2
Diploma: Unit 6: 1.2

(Task 2b)

The table below lists different types of relationship. For each type, write what the relationship is. An example has been completed for you.

Relationship type	Example
Supervisory	e.g. Me and my manager
Colleagues	
Between teams	
Between professionals	
With others	

ERR/WorkSkills: Unit 3: 1.1, 1.2, 1.3, 1.4

Task 2c

i) Below are some case studies of problems at work. Select the aspect of employment law that each one relates to from this list.

Aspects of employment law:

- discrimination
- working hours
- holiday
- sickness absence and sick pay
- data protection
- health and safety.

1 Salina was told that because of staffing shortages she would be expected to cut short her holiday this year.

Aspect of employment law: _____

_____

2 Although he was more experienced, Marc believes that he did not get promotion because of his sexual orientation.

Aspect of employment law: _____

_____

3 Melanie has not yet attended the moving and handling of people training but has been asked to help someone with limited mobility into their bed from a chair.

Aspect of employment law: _____

_____

4 Gina overheard staff discussing private information about her which she had shared with her supervisor.

Aspect of employment law: _____

_____

1

ii)   List the main features of current employment legislation:

- _____

- _____

- _____

- _____

iii) Complete the following sentence:

Employment legislation exists because ...

_____

_____

PLTS: IE3   iv)   What kinds of information and support are there to help you with Employment Rights and Responsibilities? Complete the list below. An example has been done for you.

- HR department

- _____

- _____

- _____

- _____

- _____

- _____

What kinds of information and support are there to help you with Employment Rights and Responsibilities?

BTEC: Unit 8: 1.2, 1.3
Diploma: Unit 8: 1.1, 1.2, 1.3

Task 3

Produce a leaflet about health and safety for new starters at your workplace. You can fill in the example shown below or do your own, following the same structure, to give to anyone starting work.

HEALTH AND SAFETY IN OUR WORKPLACE

There are many pieces of legislation that relate to health and safety. The main ones include:
- Health and Safety at Work Act 1974
-
-
-

The main points of health and safety procedures that affect you are:
- Dealing with accidents and injuries
-
-
-

Everybody in the workplace has responsibility for health and safety.

You	Your Employer	Others
Look after your own health and safety	Provide training where necessary	Look after their own health and safety

1

BTEC: Unit 6: 2.2, 2.3
WorkSkills: Unit 1: 1.3

(Task 4)

(Task 4a)

It is important to be clear about the agreed ways of working in your organisation.

i) Using the table below, complete the list of the documents that set out details of your employment. For each document on the list state where it is stored and how it can be accessed.

Your assessor may ask to see the documents on their visit but you do not have to photocopy them.

The list has been started for you. Fill in the blank spaces with any other documents. Exactly which documents are included on your list will depend on your organisation. It might include any of the following:

- health and safety policy and procedures
- equality and diversity policy
- policy on confidentiality and data protection
- policy on harassment, bullying and conflict management.

Documents setting out relationship with employer	Where they are stored/how to access
Job description	Company website/from HR page
Grievance procedure	
Employee handbook	
Contract of employment	
Apprenticeship Agreement	

ii) Why is it important that you have access to up-to-date versions of these documents?

_____

_____

iii) What is the purpose of the Apprenticeship Agreement?

_____

_____

ERR/WorkSkills: Unit 3: 2.1

Task 4b

Complete the following information about your role.

My working hours are:

_____

_____

My place of work is:

_____

_____

If I cannot attend work I should:

_____

_____

If I am sick I should:

_____

_____

If I am still sick after ..... days I should:

_____

_____

If I continue to be sick my employer will:

_____

_____

My sick pay entitlement is:

_____

_____

My notice period is:

_____

_____

1

My probationary period lasts for:

_____

_____

During probation, my notice period is:

_____

_____

BTEC: Unit 2: 1.1,1.3
Unit 6: 2.2
Diploma: Unit 2: 1.2. 1.3
ERR/WorkSkills Unit 3: 2.5

(Task 4c)

Complete the following examples to show how and when you have complied with policies and procedures in your workplace:

i) To maintain my organisation's **good reputation** I have:

_____

_____

If I do not do this the consequence is:

_____

_____

ii) To comply with my organisation's **health and safety** policy and procedure, I have:

_____

_____

If I do not comply the consequence is:

_____

_____

iii) To comply with my organisation's **equality and diversity** policy and procedure, I have:

_____

_____

1

If I do not comply the consequence is:

_____

_____

iv) To comply with my organisation's **confidentiality and data protection** policy and procedure, I have:

_____

_____

If I do not comply the consequence is:

_____

_____

v) To comply with my organisation's policy on **harassment, bullying and conflict management** I have:

If I do not comply the consequence is:

_____

_____

vi) Ways in which I make sure that my personal attitudes or beliefs do not affect how I work with people using my services or with my colleagues include:

- Reflecting on my own work

- _____

- _____

- _____

- _____

1

ERR/WorkSkills: Unit 3: 2.4

Task 4d

i)   What personal information should you keep up to date with your employer?

 • Phone number

 • _____

 • _____

 • _____

 • _____

 • _____

ii)   Why does your employer need to have this up-to-date information?

_____

_____

BTEC: Unit 6: 2.1
Diploma: Unit 2: 1.1
Unit 6: 2.1
ERR/WorkSkills: Unit 3: 3.1, 3.2, 3.3, 3.4

Task 4e

i)   What is your role?

You need to show that you understand what your job description means for you.

Where there are job titles (for example reports to ... , responsible for ...) you need to list the names of the actual people.

Where it lists your duties, provide an example of what you should do.

You can either write the information on a copy of your job description or complete the table below.

The job description says ...	What this means is ...

1

ii) How does your role help to improve the service provided for the people who use your organisation?

_____

_____

iii) Complete the spider diagram below to show how your role links to the wider sector. An example is completed for you.

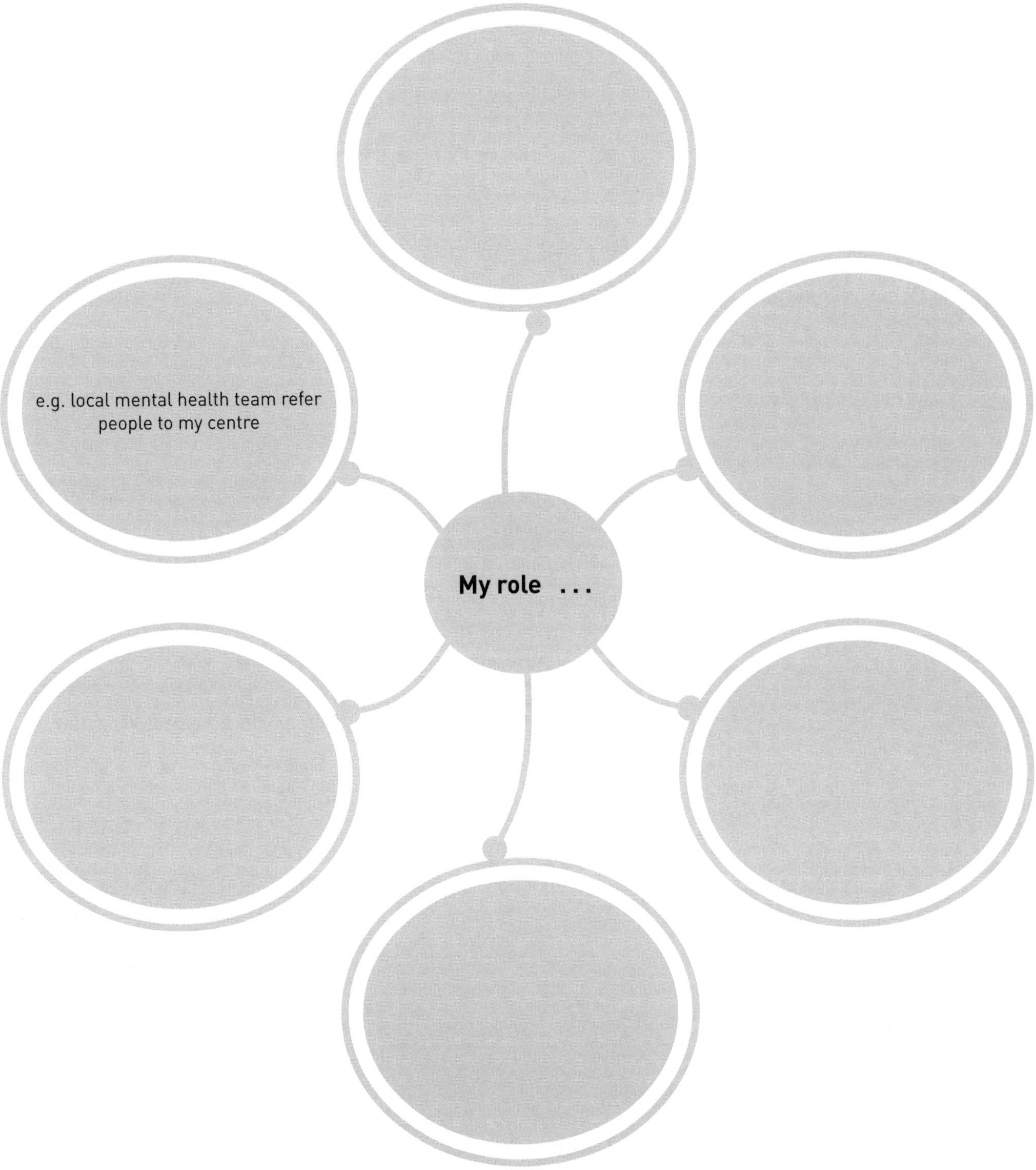

e.g. local mental health team refer people to my centre

My role . . .

1

iv) The table below lists some of the representative bodies in the health and social care sector. Complete the table showing their roles and responsibilities.

Representative body	Role in the sector
UNISON	
Skills for Care and Development	
British Association of Social Workers	
Care Quality Commission	
Criminal Records Bureau	

v) Why is it important that you do not carry out tasks which are not part of your own job description?

_____

_____

ERR/WorkSkills: Unit 3: 2.3

(Task 4f)

i) What happens when things go wrong?

Give **an example** of something that could be handled within the grievance procedure:

_____

_____

_____

ii) Look at the grievance policy of your organisation. Do a flow chart to show each step of the process that should be taken. You may add more boxes if you wish.

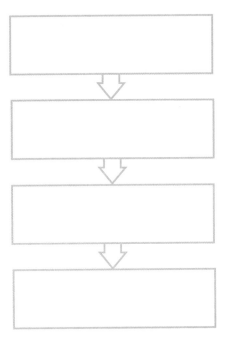

ERR/WorkSkills: Unit 3: 2.2

Task 4g

Do you know where your money goes?

Annotate one of your pay statements with an explanation of what each section covers.

Task 5

Diploma: Unit 4: 1.1
PLTS: IE1

Task 5a

Duty of care is an important idea when working in health and social care.

Choose which of the statements below you think are true.

1 a) Duty of care is a legal obligation.

  b) Duty of care is not a legal obligation.

2 a) You are required to work in the best interests of the person using the service.

  b) You are required to work in the best interests of the service provider.

3 a) You must carry out care only within the limits of your role.

  b) You must carry out any type of care the individual requests.

15

1

Diploma: Unit 4: 1.2
PLTS: IE2, IE6, EP3, EP4

Task 5b

Complete the spider diagram below showing how duty of care affects your own role:

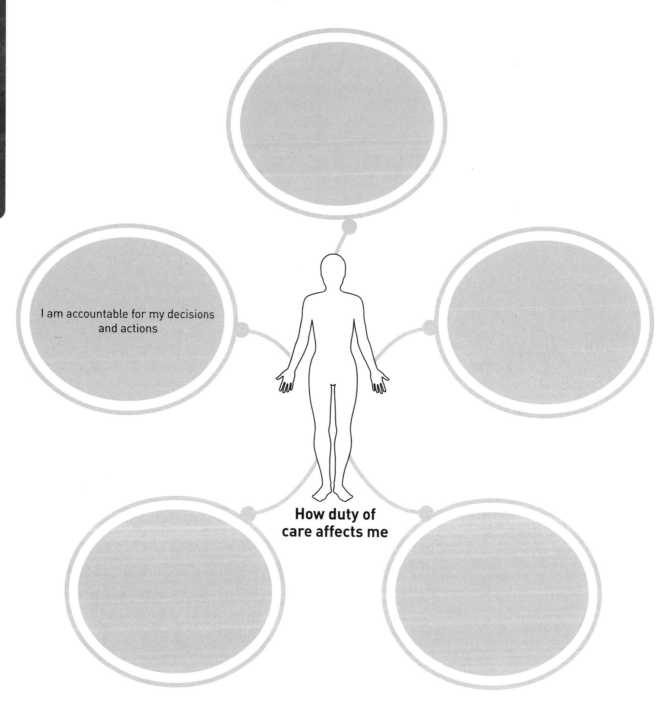

I am accountable for my decisions and actions

How duty of care affects me

Diploma: Unit 4: 2.1, 2.2

Task 5c

i) Sometimes you will come across problems where an individual's wishes go against your duty of care for them. For example, an individual may want to do something that could cause them harm. Write down an example of when this has happened in your workplace.

Remember that in order to meet confidentiality requirements you must not include any information which will identify individuals.

_____

_____

_____

ii) When you have a problem like this, there are many places you can go for advice and support. List three of them below.

1. _____

2. _____

3. _____

ERR/WorkSkills: Unit 3: 5.1, 5.2, 5.3, 5.4

Task 6

i) The health and social care sector is often in the news. List three occasions when concerns have been raised about the sector. Check in newspapers or on the internet.

- _____

- _____

- _____

ii) For one of your examples, fill in the table below showing how three different people might feel about the event.

Management of the service involved	Relative of the person involved	Person who works at the service involved (for example care worker)

iii) How do you think negative coverage of the health and social care sector changes the views of the public about the sector?

_____

_____

_____

a) Do they feel more or less positive about people who work in the sector?

_____

_____

_____

_____

b) Are they happy with the service they or their relatives are receiving?

_____

_____

_____

_____

iv) Have public concerns about the health and social care sector and the way services are delivered made any changes to your workplace?

_____

_____

_____

_____

BTEC: Unit 2: 1.2, 2.1, 3.1, 3.3
Diploma: Unit 2: 2.1, 3.1
PLTS: CT6, RL5, CT3

(Task 7)

i) It is important to consider your personal development.

Throughout your Apprenticeship, your assessor and manager will encourage you to think about or reflect on what you do at work.

How can reflection help you to develop your knowledge and skills?

_____

_____

_____

_____

It is important to consider your personal development

ii) Describe a learning activity that improved your own knowledge, skills and understanding.

_____

_____

_____

_____

iii) What did you learn?

_____

_____

_____

_____

iv) Where can you go for support in your learning and development?

_____

_____

_____

_____

v) This is a template for a Personal Development Plan. Below it are statements about what you should put in different sections. Match each statement to the correct section of the plan.

Personal Development Plan		Name:			
1. Review of strengths and weaknesses relevant to current and future roles	**2.** Learning topic to be targeted in the plan and how the learning will be used	**3.** Knowledge to be learnt	**4.** Skills to be learnt and developed	**5.** Learning activities and dates	**6.** Assessment and dates

Insert the number of the correct section of the plan next to each description.

☐ *This space should include a brief description of the area the person will be trying to develop and what difference the learning could make to their role.*

☐ *This space should include detailed information about which skills the person will develop. Objectives should be SMART (specific, measurable, achievable, realistic and time-bound).*

☐ *This space should include a description of what the person does well and where they do less well in the job. It should be based on evidence. It should identify changes in the job and possible changes in career and the relevant strengths and weaknesses of the individual.*

☐ *This space should include target dates for achievement and space for the comments of the person and their manager to assess the success of different objectives.*

☐ *This space should include detailed information about what knowledge the person will gain. Objectives should be SMART (specific, measurable, achievable, realistic and time-bound).*

☐ *This space should include a description of any learning activities the person will do, what knowledge and skills they will gain and when the activities will take place.*

You will need to complete your own personal development plan. If your workplace does not have its own template, you may want to use the one above. You should complete the plan together with your manager.

1

BTEC: Unit 2: 3.2, 3.4
Diploma: Unit 2: 2.2, 3.2
WorkSkills: Unit 1: 2.1, 2.3
Unit 9: 1.1, 1.2, 2.1, 2.2, 2.3, 2.4 2.5
PLTS: EP4

EVIDENCE GATHERING

In this activity you will identify an area of your work that will capture evidence of how you operate as a team leader. *Your assessor will help you to identify suitable items of evidence.*

You need to gather evidence of activity within areas of your work to demonstrate:

that you can complete a personal development plan and assess your own knowledge and skills.

Suggested evidence may include:

- completed personal development plan
- diary or reflective account of your own learning
- witness testimony from manager about your participation in the process of building a personal development plan.

Your assessor may wish to ask you some follow-up questions on the personal development plan process. These may include the following:

- How should you agree a personal development plan?
- What are the benefits of a personal development plan?
- Why should you meet deadlines and be organised?
- How has a learning activity improved your knowledge, skills and understanding?
- What happens if you do not complete learning on time?

Being able to contribute to the health and safety of your workplace and to safeguard the people around you is an important part of your role as a health and social care worker.

In this section you will find a range of activities to help you prepare and gather evidence for your assessment related to the following topics:

1. Health and safety

2. Safeguarding

The practical observation within this visit takes the form of a guided tour that you give your assessor around your workplace. You will need to make sure that you will be able to have some time away from your usual duties to spend with your assessor. You should discuss this with your supervisor when arranging the date of your assessor's visit.

23

2

1. HEALTH AND SAFETY

This sequence of activities will allow you to demonstrate your knowledge of health and safety policies and procedures in your workplace. As a health and social care worker, it is important that you are competent in assessing risks and hazards and implementing good practice on health and safety.

KNOWLEDGE AND UNDERSTANDING

These activities assess your knowledge of health and safety. There are different items of legislation that you must know about as well as the policies of your own workplace.

Task 1

This task will enable you to demonstrate that you understand which tasks in your setting carry health and safety risks and how you should approach such tasks. You should include tasks that require moving and handling of equipment and other objects.

BTEC: Unit 8: 1.1, 1.4, 5.1, 5.3
Diploma: Unit 8: 1.4, 1.5, 5.1
PLTS: IE1

Task 1a

Please complete the table below listing the tasks in your setting which carry health and safety risks, identifying which require specialist training and which legislation is relevant. The first line gives you an example.

Task which carries health and safety risks	Requires specialist training?	Relevant legislation and regulations
Cleaning the floor	Yes	Control of Substances Hazardous to Health (COSHH) Regulations 2002

BTEC: Unit 8: 5.2
Diploma: Unit 8: 5.2

(Task 1b)

Complete the spider diagram below with the principles for safe moving and handling. Give a principle in each box.

2

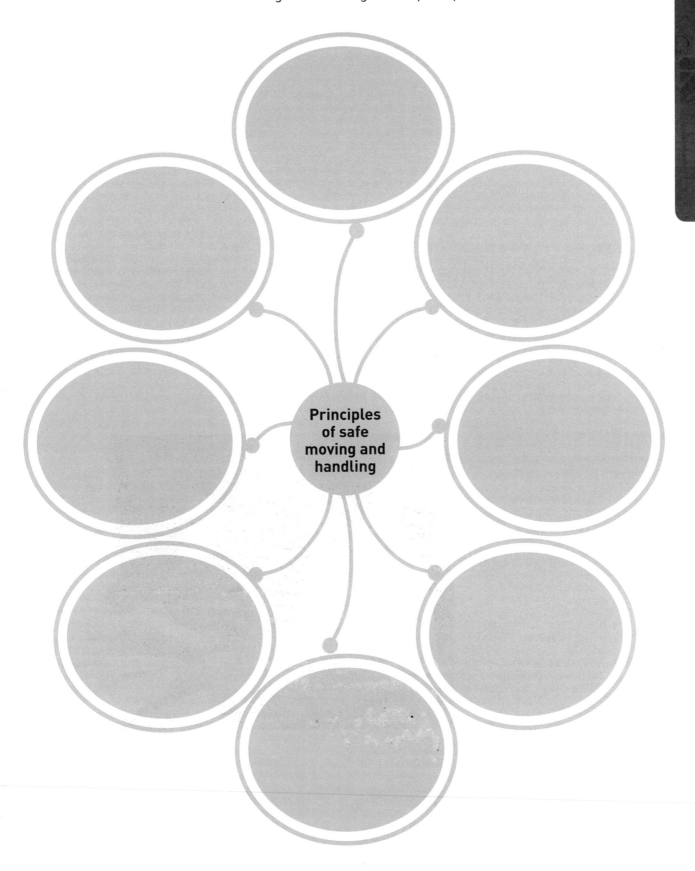

2

BTEC: Unit 8: 1.5
PLTS: IE1, CT4

Task 1c

It can be important to find out more information and gain additional support relating to health and safety matters. How do you do this?

Please complete the box below.

How I access additional support and information relating to health and safety is:

_____

_____

_____

_____

Task 2

This task is designed to help you demonstrate that you know and understand the meaning of 'hazard' and 'risk', why it is important to assess the risks in your workplace and how and when to report potential risks that you have identified.

You need to demonstrate that you know and understand the meaning of 'hazard' and 'risk'

BTEC: Unit 8: 2.1, 2.2, 2.3
Diploma: Unit 8: 2.1, 2.2, 2.3
PLTS: EP1

Task 2a

You are asked to produce notes that would be helpful to a new starter, setting out information on hazards and risk assessment.

Complete the box on the following page.

A hazard means ...

and examples of hazards in our workplace are ...

Risk means ...

and examples of risks in our workplace are ...

It is important to assess risks because ...

If I have a dilemma about people's rights and health and safety, a risk assessment can help by ...

I need to report potential risks within ...

The people I report to are ...

To report the potential risks I use ...

2

BTEC: Unit 8: 3.1, 3.2, 3.3, 5.3
Diploma: Unit 8: 3.1, 3.2
PLTS: IE1, SM3, EP1, EP2

Task 2b

i) Complete the spider diagram below for your workplace, to show the different types of accident or sudden illness that can take place.

In the space on the next page, outline the procedure to follow in each case.

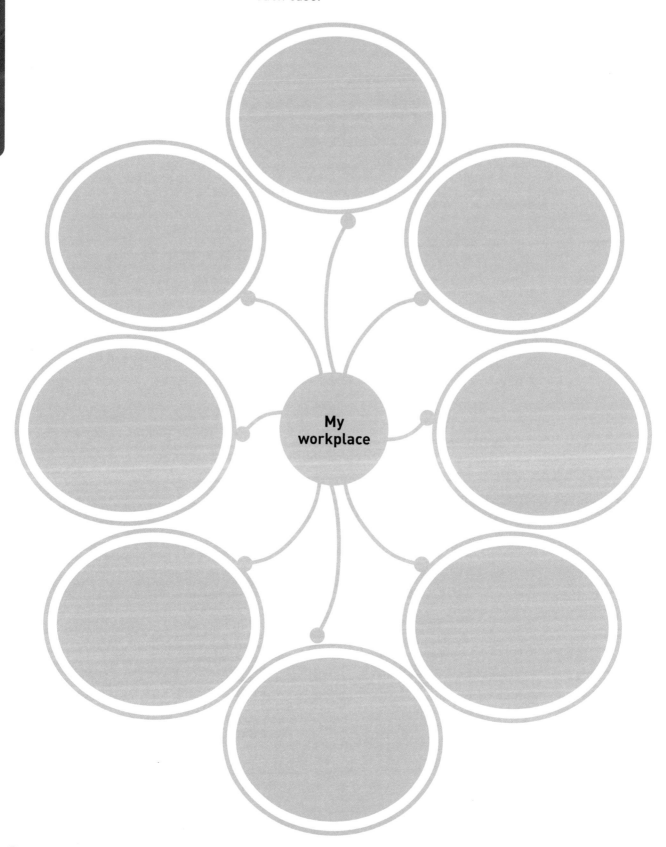

My workplace

2

ii) In some of the boxes above you may have identified that first aid should be undertaken. Why should first aid only be carried out by someone with specialist training?

iii) Why is specialist training also necessary for tasks involving moving and handling?

2

BTEC: Unit 8: 7.1, 7.2, 6.1, 8.2
Diploma: Unit 8: 6.1, 6.2, 7.1, 7.2, 7.3, 8.1, 8.2, 8.3
Unit 58: 2.3
PLTS: IE1, CT1

PUTTING IT INTO PRACTICE

This activity will enable your assessor to examine your competence by observing you carrying out workplace activities. This might include asking related questions to test your underpinning knowledge.

Guided tour of your workplace

You will be asked to walk your assessor through your workplace showing them how a number of health and safety issues are managed. If you are short of time, your assessor may ask you to produce annotated digital photographs of the parts of your workplace mentioned below, rather than including them in your tour. Prepare yourself to show your assessor the following:

- arrangements for maintaining security for access to the premises
- checking the identity of visitors and people who ask for information
- recording who is on the premises
- how you protect yourself, work colleagues and others
- where the hazardous substances are stored and disposed
- what are the safe evacuation routes and how people are guided and supported to them
- how you move and handle things safely
- where medication is kept in your workplace.

Questions you are likely to be asked could include the following:

- What are the agreed ways of working for allowing people access and checking their identity?
- How do you use hazardous substances so that safe practice is followed?
- How would you respond to specific emergencies in different parts of the premises?
- How is medication handled in your workplace and by whom?
- If you have concerns about the safety or hygiene of equipment or facilities, how should you report them?

2. SAFEGUARDING

As a health and social care worker you have an important role in protecting individuals from harm and abuse. You must also be able to look after your own well-being and that of others.

KNOWLEDGE AND UNDERSTANDING

These activities assess your knowledge and understanding of things that affect your own well-being as well as the policies and legislation concerning abuse.

Task 1

It is important to maintain your own well-being and to avoid stress when you are working in a health and social care environment.

BTEC: Unit 8: 9.1
Diploma: Unit 8: 9.1
PLTS: IE1

Task 1a

Using the diagram below, identify common signs and symptoms that may indicate that a person is experiencing stress. An example has been completed for you.

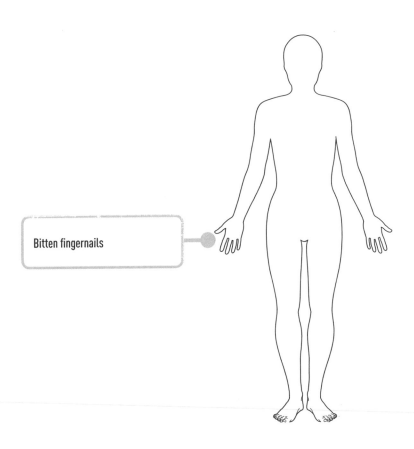

Bitten fingernails

2

BTEC: Unit 8: 9.2, 9.3
Diploma: Unit 8: 9.2, 9.3,
Unit 55: 2.4

Task 1b

It is important that you recognise what makes you stressed and how you can manage your own stress. Using the table below, write down all the situations that trigger a stressful response in you and then write how you manage your stress, including what sources of support you have at work.

Triggers of stress	How I manage stress	Who can help?
Heavy workload	Careful planning	My supervisor

Diploma: Unit 55: 1.4

Task 1c

Anni provides care for Daniel, a young adult with a disability following a car accident. Daniel is angry and distressed because he can no longer participate in the sporting activities he loves.

How might this situation impact on Anni's well-being?

- _____

- _____

- _____

WorkSkills: Unit 9: 1.4, 1.5

Task 1d

i) It is important for your well-being to achieve a good work-life balance. Fill in the planner below for your week to show how you balance your work and personal life.

	Morning	Afternoon	Evening
Monday			
Tuesday			
Wednesday			
Thursday			
Friday			
Saturday			
Sunday			

ii) Having a good relationship with your peers will help you to achieve your learning goals. Write down an example of how a relationship with one of your peers has helped you succeed.

_____

_____

_____

_____

_____

2

You need to identify common signs and indicators of stress

Task 2

Safeguarding vulnerable adults is an important part of working in a health and social care setting. You need to know about different types of abuse, the details of serious case reviews when things go wrong, national and local safeguarding policies and systems and the types of agencies involved in safeguarding and their roles.

BTEC: Unit 4: 1.1, 1.2
Diploma: Unit 5: 1.1, 1.2

Task 2a

Prepare a series of flash cards aimed at helping a new member of staff that describes different types of abuse including:

- physical abuse
- sexual abuse
- emotional/psychological abuse
- financial abuse
- institutional abuse
- self neglect
- neglect by others.

Set out each card like the example on the next page. For each type of abuse, you should first of all define the type of abuse and then go on to identify signs and symptoms associated with that particular type of abuse.

2

Type of abuse:

_____

_____

Definition:

_____

_____

_____

Signs and symptoms:

_____

_____

_____

_____

_____

_____

BTEC: Unit 4: 3.3
Diploma: Unit 5: 3.3

(Task 2b)

You need to know about what happens when things go wrong.

In the table below list recent serious case reviews and the name of the individual who was the subject of the original case.

Serious Case Review	Individual

BTEC: Unit 4: 3.1
Diploma: Unit 5: 3.1

Task 2c

There are different national and local policies and systems that are involved in safeguarding.

Sort the following list into:

    1 national policies

    2 local systems

relating to safeguarding.

Write national or local next to each policy or system:

- Independent Safeguarding Authority (ISA)
- Local Safeguarding Children Boards (LSCBs)
- 'Every Child Matters' (2003)
- employer/organisational policies and procedures
- Vetting and Barring Scheme (VBS)
- Criminal Record Bureau (CRB)
- Common Assessment Framework (CAF)
- Local Area Agreements (LAAs)
- 'No Secrets' framework and codes of practice for health and social care (2000)
- 'Safeguarding Adults' policy review (2009)
- Care Quality Commission; 'Working Together to Safeguard Children' (2006)
- multi-agency adult protection arrangements
- Local Safeguarding Adults Boards (LSABs) and protection committees.

BTEC: Unit 4: 3.2
Diploma: Unit 5: 3.2
PLTS: IE3

(Task 2d)

For each occupation or organisation identified in the table, describe their role in safeguarding.

Sector	Role		
Health Services	GP:	Nurse:	Health visitor:
Social Services	Social worker:	Care assistant:	Residential worker:
Third Sector (Voluntary)	MIND:	NSPCC:	Age UK:

BTEC: Unit 4: 1.3, 2.1, 2.2, 2.3, 3.4, 4.1, 4.2, 5.1, 5.2, 5.3
Diploma: Unit 5: 1.3, 2.1, 2.2, 2.3, 3.4, 4.1, 4.2, 5.1, 5.2, 5.3
PLTS: IE1, IE3, IE5, EP1, EP2, EP3, EP5, CT1

PROFESSIONAL DISCUSSION

Your assessor will conduct a professional discussion with you, which will capture evidence necessary to prove your level of knowledge and understanding of topic areas.

Below are some topic areas you will need to consider when preparing for the professional discussion with your assessor.

- How the likelihood of abuse can be reduced.

- What to do when abuse is suspected or alleged.

Your assessor will plan the content of your professional discussion and will advise you to help you to prepare beforehand. The professional discussion may cover more than this section of your Workbook.

2

Discussion process

The discussion process will offer you the opportunity to show that you know the factors underlying abuse, how to respond to abuse and how to minimise the chances of abuse occurring.

To prepare for your professional discussion, you should think about how you could answer questions such as the following.

- How can working with person-centred values reduce the likelihood of abuse?

- How could active participation reduce the likelihood of abuse?

- How would you promote choice and rights to reduce the likelihood of abuse?

- Why do you think an accessible complaints procedure is important?

- Explain the roles the different agencies have that are part of the safeguarding procedures.

- Name some reports that identify failings to protect individuals from abuse.

- Where can you get information about your own role in relation to safeguarding and protecting individuals from abuse?

- What are unsafe practices and what should you do if they are identified?

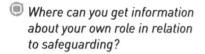

Where can you get information about your own role in relation to safeguarding?

This visit has the broad theme of communication. Within the health and social care environment you will come across many individuals who rely on your effective communication skills to help them get through the day. This is an enormous responsibility, which is why communication skills will also be assessed on other visits.

In this section you will find a range of activities to help you prepare and gather evidence for your assessment related to the following topic:

➔ 1. Communication and handling information

Before your assessor's visit you will need to complete the tasks and gather the evidence required. The assessment and care planning evidence that you gather needs to show the things set out in the Assessment Workbook: your organisation may well already require you to comply with this sort of practice. If it does not, you will need to ensure that your evidence does show what is asked for in the Assessment Workbook.

In responding to any of the knowledge tasks you should make sure that all the examples you use are anonymous.

The practical observation in this section will assess your communication skills as you implement a care plan. You should discuss this with your supervisor and assessor before you arrange the visit.

3

1. COMMUNICATION AND HANDLING INFORMATION

The activities in this sequence assess your knowledge and competence in communication, including working with those with sensory loss. If you are not taking the unit on sensory loss, your assessor may guide you to omit some of the activities that focus on this area.

KNOWLEDGE AND UNDERSTANDING

These activities assess your knowledge of communication and how to handle information.

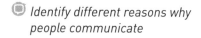

Identify different reasons why people communicate

BTEC: Unit 1: 1.1, 2.2
Diploma: Unit 1: 1.1

(Task 1)

(Task 1a)

Complete the spider diagram showing why people communicate.
Under each entry, list a method of communication you could use.
An example has been completed for you.

3

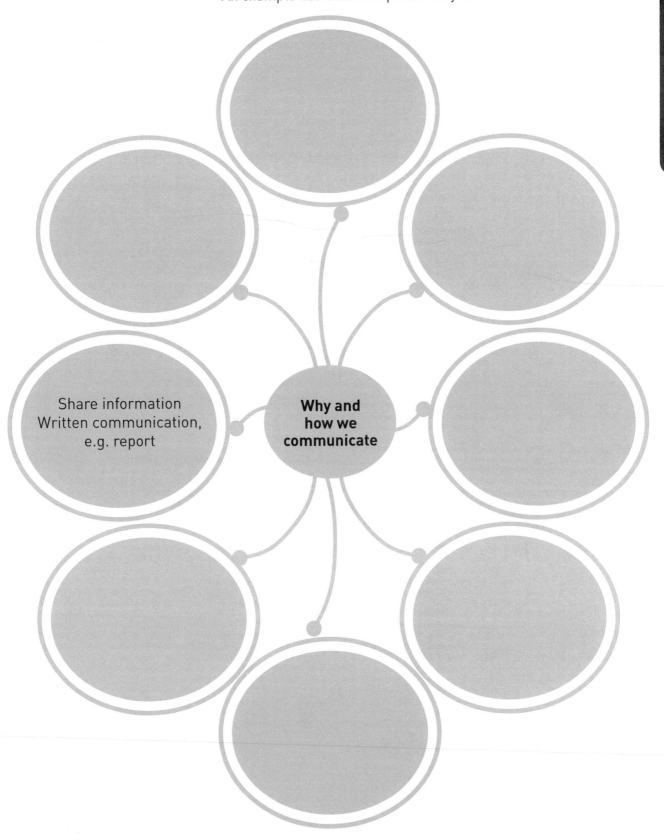

3

BTEC: Unit 1: 1.2, 2.1, 3.1, 3.2
Diploma: Unit 1: 1.2, 3.1
PLTS: EP4, CT4, RL5, RL6, IE1, IE3, IE4, IE5, CT1

Task 1b

Write a leaflet for new starters about communication in your workplace. Follow the structure provided below.

COMMUNICATION

In our workplace effective communication affects all aspects of our work. The different people we communicate with are . . .

-
-
-
-

We need to communicate effectively with them to . . .

-
-
-
-

It is important to find out an individual's communication preferences, needs and wishes because . . .

-
-
-

You will often find barriers to communication. Below are some suggestions for reducing these barriers and making communication better.

Barrier to communication	Reducing the barrier
Sensory impairment (e.g. deafness)	Hearing aid/using sign language/ reduce background noise

Ways you can check that comunication has been understood include:

-
-
-

Diploma: Unit 34: 1.1, 1.2, 1.3, 1.4, 2.2, 4.1

Task 1c

i)   Sensory loss can be a barrier to communication.

Complete the table below to show the signs and indicators of sensory loss.

Type of sensory loss	Signs and indicators
Sight loss	
Hearing loss	
Deafblindness	

ii) There are many different factors which can have a positive and negative impact on individuals with sensory loss, including the attitudes and beliefs of others.

Complete the table below.

Factor	Positive impact	Negative impact	To overcome negative factors
Methods of communication			
Layout of environment			
Routines			
Aids to mobility			

iii) How can the attitudes and beliefs of others disable individuals with sensory loss?

How can these attitudes be overcome?

Complete the diagram below – an example has been done for you.

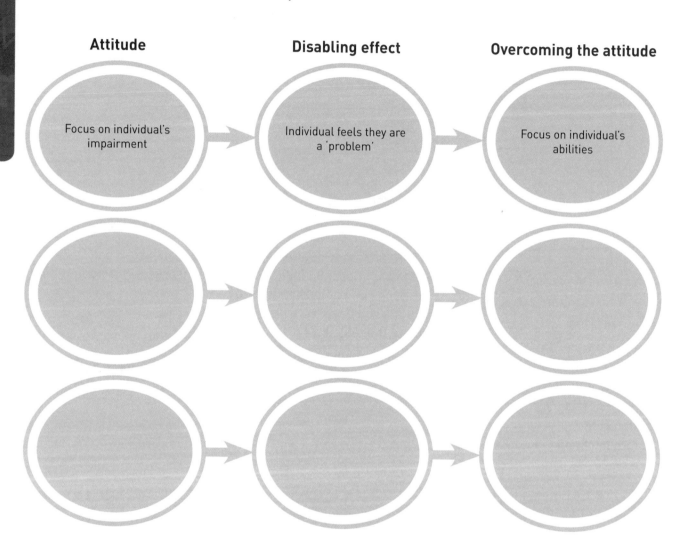

Attitude

Disabling effect

Overcoming the attitude

Focus on individual's impairment

Individual feels they are a 'problem'

Focus on individual's abilities

iv) How can you make a difference to individuals with sensory loss when you communicate? Write this here.

_____

_____

_____

Task 2

Task 2a

i) What is the meaning of confidentiality?

_____

_____

_____

ii) In what kind of situations might you need to breach normal rules about confidentiality of information?

• _____

• _____

• _____

iii) How do you maintain confidentiality in your day-to-day communication?

List four things that you do.

1 _____

2 _____

3 _____

4 _____

Task 2b

There are several pieces of legislation that relate to the recording, storage and sharing of information in health and social care. Circle the key piece of legislation below that covers this area.

Health and Safety at Work etc. Act 1974

Data Protection Act 1998

Local Authority Social Services Act 1970

Equality Act 2010

Misuse of Drugs Act 1971

Care Standards Act 2000

3

How do you maintain confidentiality in your day-to-day communication?

BTEC: Unit 9: 1.2, 2.2
Diploma: Unit 9: 1.2, 2.2
PLTS: IE1, IE2, IE3, EP4

Task 2c

Write a notice to put up next to where information is sorted in your workplace. It should follow the format below.

Why we have secure systems to record and store information:

- _____

- _____

- _____

What you should do if you are concerned about the way information is being handled:

- _____

- _____

- _____

EVIDENCE GATHERING

In this activity you will identify an area of your work that will capture evidence of how you work with your manager, colleagues and others. *Your assessor will help you to identify suitable items of evidence.*

You need to gather evidence of activity within areas of your work to demonstrate:

Diploma: Unit 3: 3.2
Unit 6: 3.4

that you have accessed information and support about diversity, equality and inclusion, partnership working and resolving conflicts appropriately.

Suggested evidence may include:

1   witness testimony from your manager or, if appropriate, from those you have contacted for information and support

2   a log or diary you have kept of when you have accessed information and support.

BTEC: Unit 7: 2.3, 5.2, 5.3
Diploma: Unit 1: 2.1, 2.2, 2.3, 3.2, 3.3, 4.2
Unit 7: 1.4
Unit 56: 1.1
Unit 6: 2.3
Unit 7: 5.2
Unit 56: 1.2, 1.3, 2.1, 2.3
PLTS: CT1, EP3, EP4, IE4

PUTTING IT INTO PRACTICE

This activity will enable your assessor to examine your competence by observing you carrying out workplace activities. This might include asking related questions to test your underpinning knowledge.

Communicating with an individual and others

This observational opportunity is designed to allow you to show how you communicate effectively with an individual and then with your colleagues and others. You should be able to complete this observation in the course of your normal duties as you implement a care plan. It may be best if the individual you choose to communicate with is someone you have not spent much time with before. You need to get the permission of the others involved for the assessor to observe you in your work tasks. As an alternative to your assessor, you may, with your assessor's agreement, arrange for an expert witness to observe and write an account of this observation.

Your assessor will want to see you communicating with the individual, with your colleagues and with others, in the best way for them. Your assessor will also be looking out for:

a) how you find out and meet the individual's needs, wishes and preferences in communication

b) how you reduce barriers to communication

c) how you check that your communication has been understood

d) how you seek advice about communication

e) how you demonstrate confidentiality when talking to your colleagues and others

f) how you take into account the individual's preferences about their care plan and the likelihood of danger or harm arising from their choices

g) how you communicate with others about the individual's care plan.

Your assessor may ask you some follow-up questions about using a care plan and risks.

3

BTEC: Unit 1: 3.4, 4.2, 4.4
Unit 6: 3.4
Unit 9: 2.1
Diploma: Unit 1: 5.4
Unit 3: 3.1
Unit 7: 1.1, 1.2, 1.3, 1.4, 1.5, 2.1, 2.2, 2.3, 2.4, 2.5
Unit 9: 2.1
PLTS: RL6, IE1, EP1, EP2, EP3, EP4

PROFESSIONAL DISCUSSION

Your assessor will conduct a professional discussion with you, which will capture evidence necessary to prove your level of knowledge and understanding of topic areas.

When preparing for the professional discussion with your assessor you will need to consider how to seek advice, support and information about a range of topics including:

- effective communication

- confidentiality

- equality, diversity and inclusion

- partnership working and resolving conflicts.

Your assessor will plan the content of your professional discussion and will advise you to help you to prepare beforehand. The professional discussion may cover more than this section of your Assessment Workbook.

Discussion process

The discussion process will offer you the opportunity to show that you know how and when to seek additional guidance and information in a variety of situations. The assessor will also wish to discuss how you have found out information and whether it was useful to you.

To prepare for your professional discussion, you should think about how you could answer questions such as the following:

- Within your workplace, who should you go to for information, advice and support?

- When should you approach someone in your organisation for information, advice and support?

- Who should you approach outside your own organisation for information, advice and support?

- When should you approach them?

- How should you find out this information from different sources?

- How useful is the information from each source?

- Is there anything you could do differently when you try to find out information in the future?

4

This visit has the broad theme of person-centred care. As a health and social care worker, the individual and their rights and choices should be at the heart of the care you provide.

In this section you will find a range of activities to help you prepare and gather evidence for your assessment related to the following topics:

➡ 1. Person-centred values in care

➡ 2. Mobility and moving

This section includes three opportunities for observation. As the first involves personal care, it will need to be assessed by someone from your workplace in advance of your assessor's visit. Discuss with your supervisor and assessor who will assess your competence in giving personal care.

Although the other two practical observations are in different streams, it is possible to run them together if your assessor agrees. The observation from the first sequence involves assisting an individual in eating and drinking and the observation from the second sequence involves supporting an individual to move. Seek guidance from your assessor about how to approach this observation opportunity before arranging when their visit is to take place.

4

1. PERSON-CENTRED VALUES IN CARE

The activities in this sequence will assess you on your knowledge of person-centred care: how you apply person-centred values in personal care, eating and drinking and care planning.

KNOWLEDGE AND UNDERSTANDING

These knowledge activities will test your understanding of person-centred values and the ideas of consent and choice.

BTEC: Unit 7: 1.1
Diploma: Unit 7: 1.1

Task 1

Task 1a

Read the statements below, then identify the one which best defines the concept of person-centred values.

1 Put the individual first in every decision you make about their care.

2 Work in partnership with individuals to ensure that their rights, independence and choices are promoted.

3 Share all information about an individual among your colleagues so you can support their needs.

BTEC: Unit 7: 1.2
Diploma: Unit 7: 1.2, 1.3
PLTS: IE3

Task 1b

Complete the spider diagram on page 51 – giving reasons why it is important to work with person-centred values, even if an individual's choices may involve risks.

BTEC: Unit 1: 1.3, Unit 7: 5.1, 5.4, Unit 8: 2.4
Diploma: Unit 1: 1.3,
Unit 7: 5.3
PLTS : RL6, IE3, EP5, CT4

Task 1c

Case study: Warren and Cara

Warren is a domiciliary care worker who has been working with Cara (aged 58) who lives alone and has been diagnosed with early onset dementia. Cara has always insisted that she wants to stay in her own home and her family agree and want her to be supported there. Warren's belief is that her needs would be better met in a residential home as he knows they have specialist support there. He has carried out a risk assessment and is concerned about Cara's health and safety, particularly when she cooks or switches on her gas fire.

1 Why is it important for Warren to observe Cara's reactions as he starts to talk about moving to a residential home?

_____

_____

continued on page 52 ⊕

4

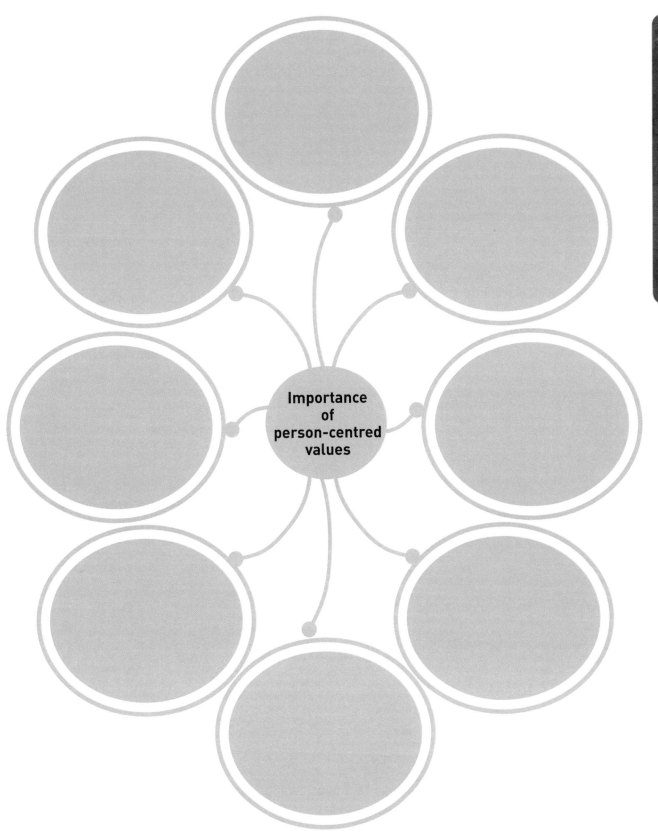

Importance
of
person-centred
values

4

2 Warren has strong opinions about fire risk as he had a family member who died in a house fire. Why is it important that he doesn't tell Cara about this?

_____

_____

3 What is the best way for Warren to support Cara? Choose two of the options below.

a) Respect Cara's decision to stay at home and stop trying to discuss a move to residential care.

b) Explore with Cara whether there are additional safety devices she could use in her home.

c) Leave information for Cara to share with her family about local residential services.

d) Contact Cara's family about her health and safety risks and ask them to persuade her to move to a residential home.

4 How can risk assessment address the dilemma between Cara's right to stay in her own home and Warren's health and safety concerns?

_____

_____

_____

_____

BTEC: Unit 7: 3.1

(Task 2)

(Task 2a)

It is important to be clear about exactly what is meant by different terms in social care.

From the list below, select the correct definition of consent:

1 Informed agreement, before making a decision or taking an action.

2 Letting an individual know what will happen next.

3 Changing a decision following a complaint about care or support.

BTEC: Unit 7: 3.2, 3.3, 3.4
Diploma: Unit 7: 3.1, 3.3
PLTS: EP1, EP2, EP3, IE5, CT4

4

Task 2b

The concept of consent is very important in health and social care.

i)   It is important to gain consent from individuals when providing care or support because ...

_____

_____

Consent can be established by ...

_____

_____

ii)   Sometimes consent cannot easily be established, perhaps because of communication difficulties or learning disabilities. In this situation you should ...

_____

_____

PLTS: CT4

Task 2c

Being able to assist individuals in challenging decisions and making complaints where necessary is an important part of your role.

i)   List three things you can do to support an individual in challenging a decision that has been made about them.

   •   _____

   •   _____

   •   _____

ii)   It is important that individuals can make complaints that are taken seriously when they are unhappy with the care or support they receive.

   Why is it important that individuals are able to do this?

_____

_____

4

iii) Fill in the boxes below with the different steps in the complaints process in your workplace.

- In Box 1 describe how a complaint can be made in your workplace.

- In Box 2 describe how a complaint is investigated in your workplace.

- In Box 3 describe how complaints are resolved in your workplace.

1
(e.g. in writing to the manager)

_____

_____

_____

2
(e.g. interviewing witnesses)

_____

_____

_____

3
(e.g. manager writes to complainant)

_____

_____

_____

iv) What is your role in the process above?

_____

_____

_____

● *Person-centred care revolves around an individual's needs, wishes and preferences*

4

EVIDENCE GATHERING

In this activity you will identify an area of your work that will capture evidence of how you operate in a health and social care setting. *Your assessor will help you to identify suitable items of evidence.*

You need to gather evidence of activity within areas of your work to demonstrate:

BTEC: Unit 7: 2.1, 2.2
Diploma: Unit 7: 2.1, 2.2
PLTS: IE5, SM7, EP6

that you understand the importance of an individual's history, preferences, wishes and needs.

To generate the evidence for these criteria, you need an individual to work with you to plan for their care and support. With your manager's agreement, you should find an individual who is prepared to work with you. You should complete the following steps.

a) Make a note of how you will find out the history, preferences, wishes and needs of the individual (e.g. one long conversation, a series of short conversations, with the individual, perhaps including their family).

4

b) Record the history, preferences, wishes and needs of the individual.

c) After your discussions, identify the changes in the care and support you give the individual and any changes to their care plan.

Suggested evidence may include:

i.   document as above recording history, needs, preferences and wishes, countersigned by your manager

ii. minutes of care plan review meeting

iii. amended care plan

iv. feedback from the individual and their family.

PUTTING IT INTO PRACTICE

These activities will assess your competence as you carry out workplace activities. You may also be asked related questions to test your underpinning knowledge.

Diploma: Unit 58: 1.1, 1.2, 1.3, 2.1, 2.2, 2.4, 2.5, 3.1, 3.2, 4.1, 4.2, 4.3, 5.2

a) Delivering personal care in a sensitive way, maintaining the dignity of the individual.

As this practical observation involves personal care, it will not be observed by your assessor but by an expert witness from your workplace.

You will be assessed on the following.

- Check with the individual that you understand their needs and preferences and that they have made an informed choice, including regarding privacy to give you consent for your actions.

- Use the correct protective equipment (including washing your hands) and explain its use to the individual.

- Prepare the facilities.

- Support the individual in personal hygiene activities (including using the toilet where necessary) and give information about how to summon help when you are out of the room. Encourage the individual to take care of their personal possessions.

- Tidy the room and dispose of waste.

Diploma: Unit 7: 3.2, 5.1
Diploma: Unit 8: 4.1, 4.2
Diploma: Unit 57: 1.1, 1.2, 2.1, 2.2, 2.3, 2.4, 3.2, 3.3, 3.4, 3.5, 4.2, 4.3, 4.4, 5.2, 5.3

b) Supporting eating and drinking.

You will be observed supporting an individual in your workplace with eating and drinking. Your assessor will want to see you do the following.

4

- Discuss with the individual the food and drink they would like and what support they need. Establish the individual's consent for any actions you may need to take.

- Prepare yourself and the individual for a meal, including where they will sit and any utensils needed.

- Assist the individual with their meal.

- Involve the individual in tidying up.

- Report and record following the procedures in your workplace.

BTEC: Unit 8: 4.1, 4.2, 4.3, 4.4
Diploma: Unit 58: 2.3
Unit 57: 1.3, 1.4, 3.1, 4.1, 5.1
PLTS: IE1, IE2, IE3

PROFESSIONAL DISCUSSION

Your assessor will conduct a professional discussion with you, which will capture evidence necessary to prove your level of knowledge and understanding of topic areas.

Below are some topic areas you will need to consider when preparing for the professional discussion with your assessor:

- safety and hygiene

- supporting eating and drinking.

Your assessor will plan the content of your professional discussion and will advise you to help you to prepare beforehand. The professional discussion may cover more than this section of your Assessment Workbook.

Discussion process

The discussion process will offer you the opportunity to show that you know about safety and hygiene and that you understand about assisting an individual with eating and drinking.

To prepare for your professional discussion, you should think about how you could answer questions such as the following.

- How do you report concerns about the safety and hygiene of equipment?

- How does infection get into the body?

- Why do you need to take care of your own health and hygiene and how should you do so?

- What difficulties might you experience relating to choice of food and drink and who could you ask for advice?

- How can you make sure that an individual has a good experience of eating and drinking?

- What could be the impact on individuals of forgetting to monitor their food and drink intake?

2. MOBILITY AND MOVING

These activities will assess your knowledge and competence in assisting individuals to move. If you are not taking both Units 46 and 68 of the Diploma, your assessor will guide you as to which parts of the Assessment Workbook you should complete.

KNOWLEDGE AND UNDERSTANDING

These knowledge activities will assess your knowledge of legislation about mobility, anatomy, health conditions affecting mobility and where you can seek advice and assistance.

BTEC: Unit 8: 6.1, 6.2
Diploma: Unit 68: 2.1, 2.2

Task 1

Think of an individual who you work with. You may wish to look at their care plan while you complete this activity. You may use examples of several individuals if you wish.

Identify the part of the care plan that refers to assisting, moving and positioning the individual. Fill in the information below for the individual you have chosen.

a) Why do you need specialist training to assist this individual to move?

_____

_____

b) What health and safety factors should you consider when moving and positioning this individual (including use of equipment)?

- _____

- _____

- _____

- _____

c) For each for the health and safety factors above, list how legislation and agreed ways of working affect your practice.

- _____

- _____

- _____

- _____

4

d) Why is it important that you follow the care plan of the individual you have identified when assisting them to move?

_____

_____

Diploma: Unit 68: 1.1

(Task 2)

It is important to know about the anatomy and physiology of the human body when you have to move and position people.

Label the diagram below. On each label include its importance in correctly moving and positioning individuals.

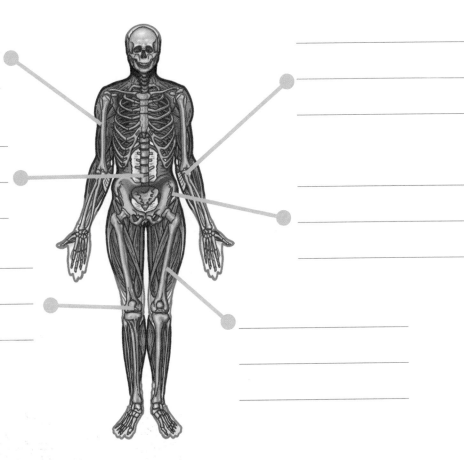

Diploma: Unit 46: 1.1, 1.2, 1.3, 1.4
Unit 68: 1.2

(Task 3)

i) Mobility is an important aspect of health and well-being.

Complete the sentence below with the definition of mobility.

Mobility is ...

_____

_____

4

ii) Using the table below, complete each column for the different conditions you have come across in your workplace. The first row has been completed for you.

Health condition	Impact on mobility, movement and positioning
Stroke	May have weakness on one side of the body, this means they may need help to stand and transfer from chair to standing.

iii) List below three benefits of maintaining and improving mobility.

- _____

- _____

- _____

BTEC: Unit 6: 3.1, 3.2, 3.3
Diploma: Unit 6: 3.1, 3.3
Unit 68: 6.1, 6.2

(Task 4)

Moving and positioning an individual is often an activity that requires you to work in partnership with others.

i) Give three reasons why it is important to work in partnership with others:

- _____

- _____

- _____

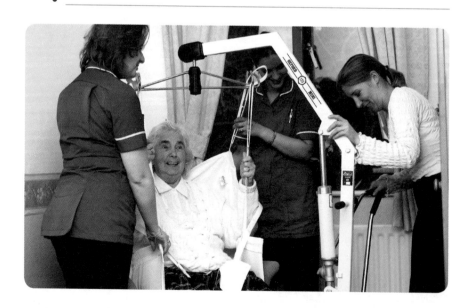

It is important to work in partnership with others

ii) Complete the spider diagram below to show ways of working that can improve partnership working and resolve conflicts.

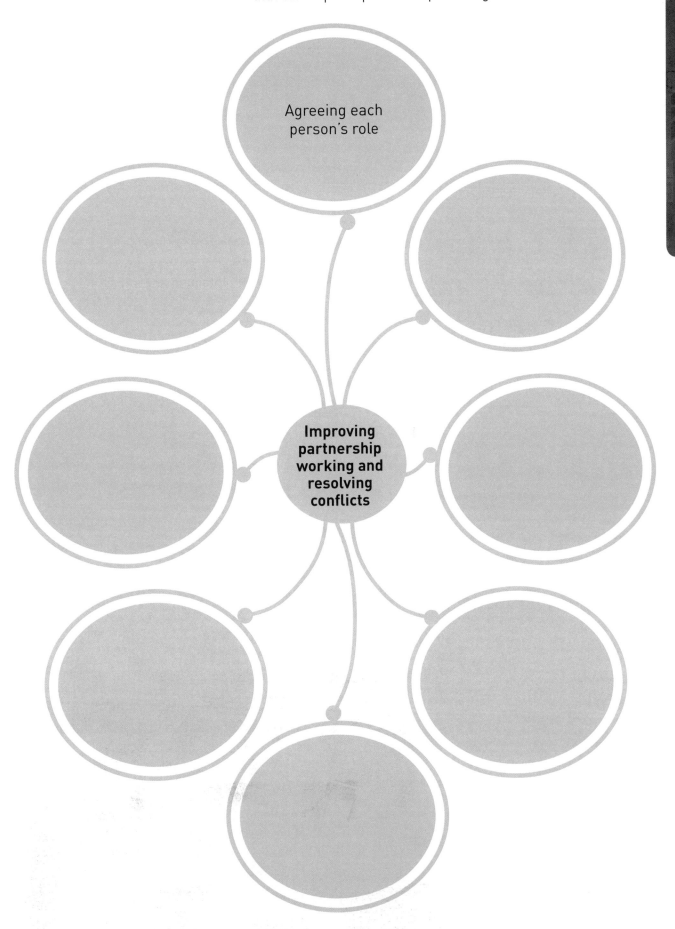

4

iii) You will sometimes find situations in which you need advice or assistance with moving an individual safely. In the table below, describe three of these situations and where you would go for advice or information.

Situation	Source of information and advice
e.g. individual complains of pain when being moved out of bed.	e.g. manager or physiotherapist

EVIDENCE GATHERING

In this activity you will identify an area of your work that will capture evidence of how you operate as a team leader. *Your assessor will help you to identify suitable items of evidence.*

You need to gather evidence of activity within areas of your work to demonstrate:

Diploma: Unit 9: 3.1, 3.2
Unit 51: 6.2
Unit 55: 5.1, 5.2
Unit 56: 3.1, 3.2
Unit 58: 6.3

a) that you can record information about an individual and their care plan.

Individuals' records that you use as evidence should be anonymised. Suggested evidence may include the following:

i.   witness testimony from your manager that you have stored and shared information appropriately

ii. an individual's care plan in which you have noted any changes in the individual's care, circumstances and mood that are relevant.

Diploma: Unit 6: 3.2
Unit 56: 4.1, 4.2, 4.3, 4.4
Unit 58: 6.1, 6.2

b) that you contribute to review and evaluation of care plans.

Individuals' records that you use as evidence should be anonymised. Suggested evidence may include the following.

i.   Witness testimony from your manager that you have sought feedback from individuals you work with about their care plan and personal care.

ii. Witness testimony from your manager about your contribution to care plan review and agreement of changes.

iii. Witness testimony from your manager that you have contributed to improved partnership working.

iv. Records showing your monitoring of the personal care you have given.

Diploma: Unit 68: 3.1, 3.2, 3.3, 3.4, 3.5, 3.6, 3.7, 4.1, 4.2, 5.1, 5.2, 5.3, 5.4, 5.5, 5.6, 5.7
Unit 46: 2.1, 2.2, 2.3, 2.4, 3.1, 3.2, 3.3, 4.1, 4.2, 4.3

PUTTING IT INTO PRACTICE

This activity will enable your assessor to examine your competence by observing you carrying out workplace activities. This might include asking related questions to test your underpinning knowledge. You may wish to link this observation to either personal care or eating and drinking.

Assisting an individual to move

This observation includes content from the units on moving and positioning an individual and assisting with mobility. If you are not taking both of these units, your assessor will guide you as to which parts of the observation to complete.

Before the observation you will need to do the following:

- Prepare by accessing up-to-date copies of information on care planning and risk assessments regarding the activity to be observed.

- Review these documents and identify actions you will need to take.

- Discuss the plan with the individual and others including resolving any disagreements.

Your assessor will observe that you can carry out the following:

- Prepare the environment.

- Check the individual is wearing suitable clothing and footwear.

- Assist the individual to move and participate actively, while communicating effectively.

- Assist the individual in using the appropriate aids.

- Monitor the individual and report on the activity, including any problems.

4

PROFESSIONAL DISCUSSION

Your assessor will conduct a professional discussion with you, which will capture evidence necessary to prove your level of knowledge and understanding of topic areas.

Below are some topic areas you will need to consider when preparing for the professional discussion with your assessor.

- How you have worked in a team to promote partnership working.

- That you agreed and completed a task within a team.

- That you took different roles in the team, depending on what needed to be done.

- What you could do better next time.

Your assessor will plan the content of your professional discussion and will advise you to help you to prepare beforehand. The professional discussion may cover more than this section of your Assessment Workbook.

Discussion process

The discussion process will offer you the opportunity to show that you have worked well within a team to promote partnership working.

To prepare for your professional discussion, you should think about how you could answer questions such as the following:

- What did you do as a team?

- What code of conduct did you agree for the team members?

- How did you complete the task?

- How did you offer and receive feedback within the team?

5

This visit has the broad themes of independence and well-being. Within the health and social care environment you will need to promote the independence and well-being of the individuals you work with.

In this final visit you will focus on one of the key principles of work in health and social care: putting the person using the service at the centre of planning and delivery. As in previous visits, at the beginning of each section this will involve finding information to complete the knowledge and understanding activities. You will already have your organisation's policies and procedures for equality and inclusion. You must now think about how these policies and procedures work in practice to celebrate diversity and ensure the well-being of individuals using your service. You will also need to demonstrate your practice when you support individuals, through evidence gathering and direct observation, so it will be beneficial if in preparation you take time to observe the practice of others when they promote independence, reflecting on how they do this.

1. INDEPENDENCE IN DAILY LIVING

The majority of this sequence is drawn from Unit 51 of the Diploma. In health and social care it is vital to promote an individual's independence as far as possible in all aspects of their life.

KNOWLEDGE AND UNDERSTANDING

These activities check your understanding of the importance of promoting independence. There is also a short activity on food safety. You must know about this if you are preparing food or helping others to prepare food.

Diploma: Unit 51: 1.1, 1.5

Task 1

Task 1a

i) In the space below outline a daily living routine for someone you know who uses health and social care services.

Daily living routine

Morning

Lunchtime

Afternoon

Evening

Night

_____

_____

_____

_____

ii) Use your information about the different daily living activities in their routine. Think about the opportunities for learning or practising new skills while carrying out these activities and describe them in the first column below. Next to each description explain the benefits. An example of a daily living activity might be to prepare a simple meal.

Opportunities for learning or practising skills	Benefits for individuals

Diploma: Unit 51: 1.6, 2.3

(Task 1b)

Complete the following statements about support for daily living.

i) It is important to establish roles and responsibilities for providing support because ...

_____

_____

_____

ii) I could receive additional guidance to resolve any difficulties or concerns about support for daily living tasks from ...

_____

_____

_____

5

BTEC: Unit 8: 11.1

Task 2

Task 2a

Food poisoning is more likely to affect people who have a lowered resistance, including older people, and those who are disabled or sick. It is important that you understand and follow the food safety standards in your health and social care setting. List the relevant legislation, guidance and policies in the space below.

_____

_____

_____

BTEC: Unit 8: 11.2, 11.3
PLTS: IE3, EP4

Task 2b

i) Look at the foods below. Think about and explain how you should store each type of food.

You should consider:

- the correct place
- the correct temperature
- the correct length of time.

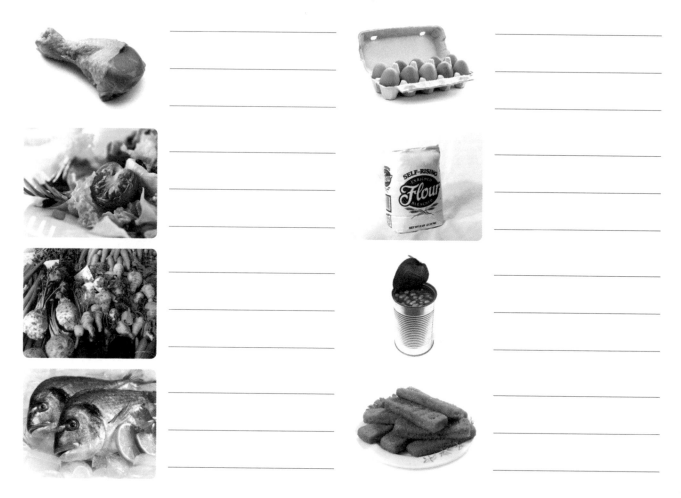

ii) You will see the terms 'Best before' and 'Use by' written on food packaging. Explain what is meant by each of the terms in the table below.

Term	Explanation
Best before	
Use by	

iii) Produce a poster which could be displayed in the kitchen of an adult care setting. The poster should include advice on:

- ways to maximise hygiene when handling food
- ways to maximise hygiene when storing food
- how food should be disposed of safely.

iv) Use the diagram below to identify common hazards when handling and storing foods. One example has been given.

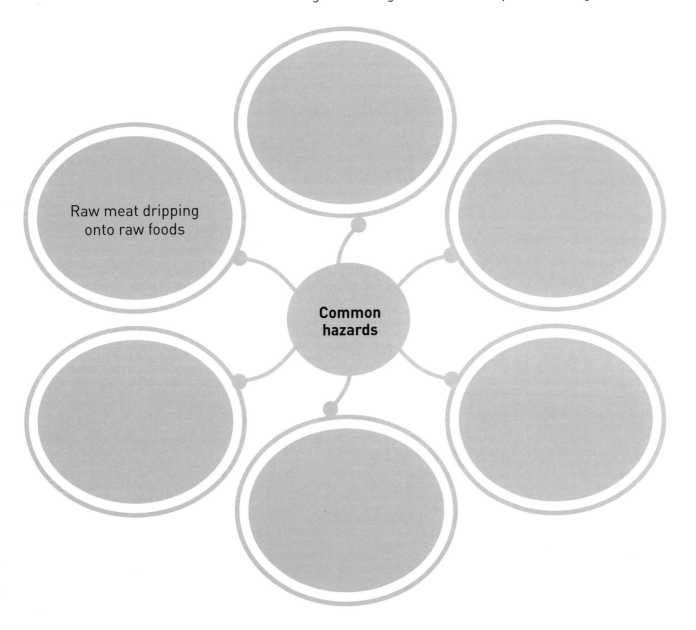

5

EVIDENCE GATHERING

In this activity you will identify an area of your work that will capture evidence of how you operate as a health and social care worker. *Your assessor will help you to identify suitable items of evidence.*

You need to gather evidence of activity within areas of your work to demonstrate:

Diploma: Unit 51: 4.1, 4.2, 4.3 **how you can assist an individual to buy, store and use household items.**

Suggested evidence may include:

i.   leaflets, printouts or catalogues showing different ways of buying household items

ii.   a log, a diary or part of a care plan showing how you have identified with an individual what household or personal items they need

iii.   witness testimony or part of a care plan showing how you have supported an individual in buying, storing and using items.

PUTTING IT INTO PRACTICE

This activity will enable your assessor to examine your competence by observing you carrying out workplace activities. This might include asking related questions to test your underpinning knowledge.

Your assessor will agree a time when they can observe you providing support to an individual with their daily living tasks in their own home. Remember that you must obtain consent from the individual and your manager for this observation to take place.

Diploma: Unit 51: 2.1, 2.2 **a) How you assess information and clarify the individual's support needs.**

Your assessor will need to see that you are able to access and use written information about the individual's support needs. They will observe how you clarify these needs with the individual and, where appropriate, significant others such as professionals or the individual's family.

Diploma: Unit 51: 3.1, 3.2, 3.3, 4.4, 4.5, 5.1, 6.1, 6.3
Unit 55: 3.1

b) How you support the individual to plan and prepare healthy meals which meet their own dietary needs.

Your assessor will observe that you encourage the individual to express their own preferences about food and prepare a simple meal. This will give you the opportunity to demonstrate respect for their dignity, culture and beliefs. They will then observe how you support the individual to use necessary items, such as food and utensils, and store them safely. You should also support the individual to clean the area independently while ensuring their safety. You must take care that you support the individual in such a way that encourages them to be as independent as possible, demonstrating that you are able to adapt your practice to address any concerns or increased independence.

Diploma: Unit 51: 5.2, 5.3
Unit 55: 3.1

c) How you approach the subject of risks to home security.

Your assessor will observe your interaction with the individual to identify and discuss any risks to their home security and agree the strategies that they are able to use to minimise the risks. For instance you might demonstrate and check that the individual is able to put on the door chain. This is a sensitive subject so you must demonstrate concern for their feelings.

BTEC: Unit 2: 2.2, 2.3
Diploma: Unit 2: 2.3, 4.2, 4.3
PLTS: IE4, RL4, RL5

PROFESSIONAL DISCUSSION

Your assessor will conduct a professional discussion with you which will capture evidence of how reflection and feedback from others has helped you to improve your knowledge, understanding and skills in different areas of your work.

Below are some topic areas you will need to consider when preparing for the professional discussion with your assessor:

- what you understand by 'reflection'
- ways that you seek feedback from others
- who has given feedback and the type of feedback given
- how reflection has helped you to improve your knowledge, understanding and skills.

Your assessor will plan the content of your professional discussion and will advise you to help you to prepare beforehand. The professional discussion may cover more than this section of your Assessment Workbook.

5

Discussion process

The discussion process will offer you the opportunity to show that you are able to reflect on your own practice and seek feedback from others such as your manager, assessor, colleagues, other professionals and people or their families using the services.

To prepare for your professional discussion, you should think about how you could answer questions such as the following:

- How often do you reflect on your own practice?

- How do you do this?

- How do you seek feedback from your manager?

- How do you seek feedback from people using the services?

- In what ways has your practice changed after reflecting on your skills?

- Has reflection changed your attitudes and what difference does this make to your work?

2. DIVERSITY

In the previous section you will have thought about how you place individuals at the centre of care planning and service delivery. Underpinning this practice is the need to promote diversity, equality and inclusion and to challenge discrimination where it exists.

You will need to show that you are able to work in an inclusive way, understanding and meeting the needs of all individuals using health and social care services. There will be a particular focus on the needs of people with sensory loss.

KNOWLEDGE AND UNDERSTANDING

This sequence of activities will help you to show evidence that you understand the concepts of diversity, equality, inclusion and discrimination and help you to identify the legislation and codes of practice which promote inclusion. You will explore how an individual's culture or background may have an effect on their daily living tasks. You must provide evidence that you know how to respect a person's individuality and promote equality and inclusion through your day-to-day work.

BTEC: Unit 3: 1.1
Diploma: Unit 3: 1.1, 1.2

(Task 1)

(Task 1a)

Write an explanation for each of the terms below.

Term	Explanation of term
Diversity	
Equality	
Inclusion	
Discrimination	

BTEC: Unit 3: 1.3
Diploma: Unit 3: 1.4
PLTS: IE3, IE6

(Task 1b)

Reflect on the information about each term and complete the sentence below.

Practices that support diversity, equality and inclusion reduce the likelihood of discrimination because ...

_____

_____

_____

_____

5

BTEC: Unit 3: 2.1, 3.1
PLTS: IE1, IE2, IE3

Task 1c

i) In the space below list the legislation and codes of practice relating to diversity, equality, inclusion and discrimination in adult social care settings.

_____

_____

_____

_____

ii) Identify sources of information, advice and support about diversity, equality, inclusion and discrimination and write your answers in the spider diagram below.

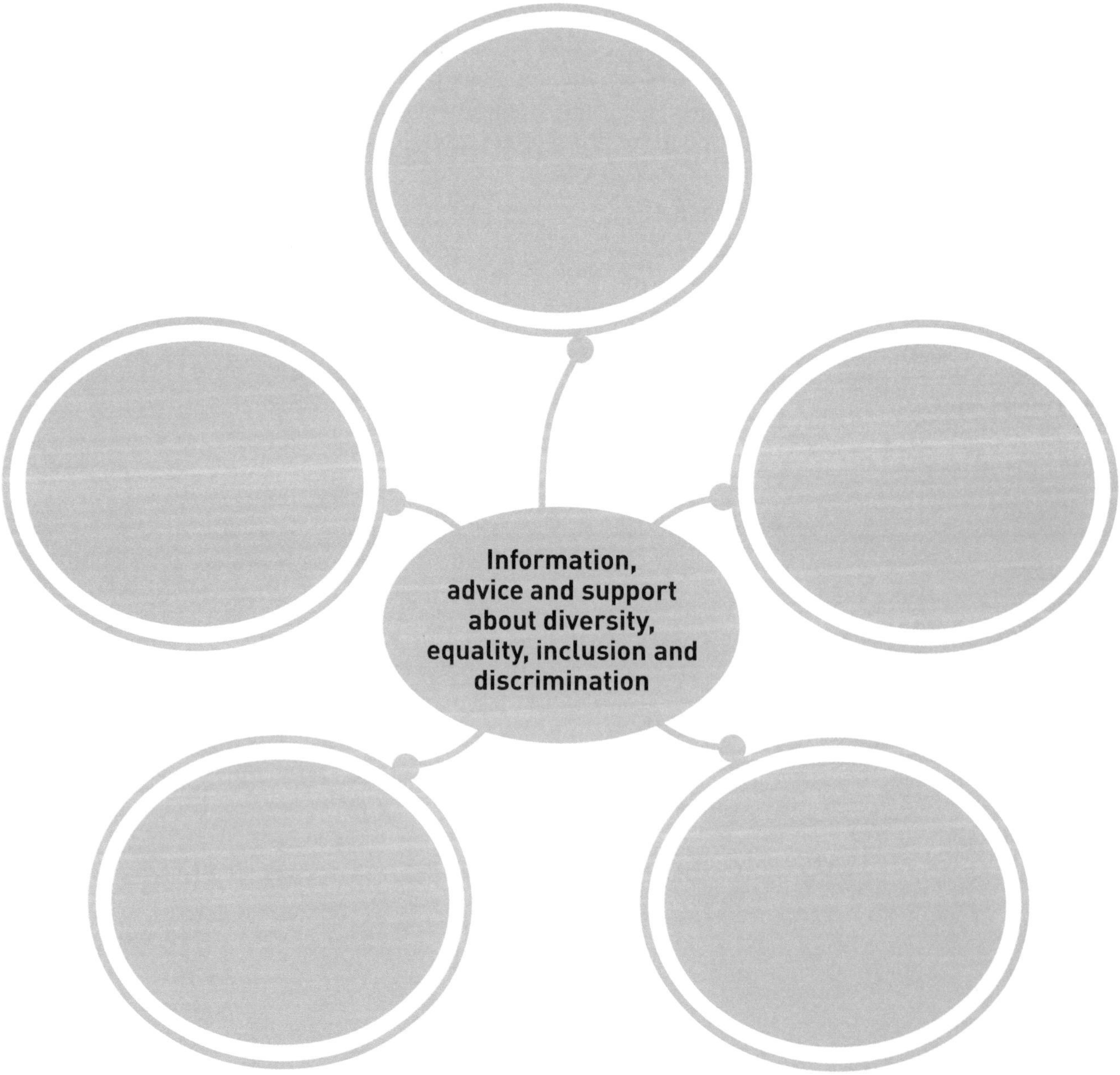

Information, advice and support about diversity, equality, inclusion and discrimination

Diploma: Unit 51: 1.3, 1.4

Task 1d

i) Give two examples of people who use health and social care services where daily living tasks may be affected by their culture or background. Write a brief description of each one in the spaces below. *Remember to observe confidentiality at all times.*

Example 1

_____

_____

_____

_____

Example 2

_____

_____

_____

_____

ii) Referring to your examples, explain the importance of providing support that respects the culture and preferences of each individual.

_____

_____

_____

_____

_____

Task 2

The following sequence of activities will support you to show that you understand the different forms of sensory loss. You will need to provide information on what must be considered when communicating with people with sensory loss and how information can be made accessible to them. You must find out about the main causes of sensory loss and the numbers of people who are affected.

5

Diploma: Unit 34: 2.1, 2.3

Task 2a

Outline what you should take into consideration when communicating with people with sight loss, hearing loss or deafblindness. Use the diagram below to record three pieces of information for each type of sensory loss.

Diploma: Unit 34: 3.1, 3.2, 3.3

Task 2b

i) Look in turn at each type of sensory loss and outline the main causes. Then explain how information can be made more accessible for them. Find out the percentage of the general population who are likely to have each form of sensory loss. Use the table opposite to record your answers.

5

Type of sensory loss	Main causes	How information can be made accessible	%
Sight loss			
Hearing loss			
Deafblindness			

ii) Complete the sentences below to explain the difference between congenital sensory loss and acquired sensory loss.

Congenital sensory loss is when ...

Acquired sensory loss is when ...

5

BTEC: Unit 3: 1.2, 2.2, 2.3, 3.2
Diploma: Unit 3: 1.3, 2.1, 2.2, 2.3
Unit 34: 4.2, 5.1
PLTS: IE3, IE4, IE5, IE6

PROFESSIONAL DISCUSSION

Your assessor will conduct a professional discussion with you which will capture evidence necessary to prove your level of knowledge and understanding of topic areas.

Below are some topic areas you will need to consider when preparing for the professional discussion with your assessor:

- the meaning of direct and indirect discrimination
- the importance of challenging discrimination
- where information and support can be obtained
- ways to show respect for others' beliefs, culture, values and preferences.

Your assessor will plan the content of your professional discussion and will advise you to help you to prepare beforehand. The professional discussion may cover more than this section of your Assessment Workbook.

Discussion process

The discussion process will offer you the opportunity to show that you understand how to work in an inclusive way and are able to seek information and support if necessary. You will also need to show that you recognise discrimination, whether intentional or inadvertent, and know how to challenge it.

To prepare for your professional discussion, you should think about how you could answer questions such as the following:

- How can you work with individuals in a way that respects their beliefs and culture?
- What action should you take if you observe that an individual is being discriminated against?
- Why might someone inadvertently discriminate against an individual?
- What do you understand by 'working in an exclusive way'?
- What action should you take if you have concerns that an individual has deteriorating hearing or sight?
- Where would you initially go to find information about sensory loss?

3. WELL-BEING

This sequence of activities will help you to provide evidence of your understanding of your role in promoting the well-being of people who use health and social care services. You must show that you understand how to recognise the signs of distress and know when intervention may be needed. This will require you to think about the links between individual identity and self esteem and well-being. You will also need to demonstrate that you can put your knowledge into practice by promoting active participation of individuals in your workplace.

KNOWLEDGE AND UNDERSTANDING

Diploma: Unit 55: 1.1, 1.2, 1.3, 2.2, 2.3

(Task 1)

i)   When working in health and social care it is important that you are sensitive to signs that an individual may be distressed. You should consider that the signs may not always be obvious and will vary between individuals. Use the image below to identify and describe signs that could indicate that a person may be distressed. You should provide information on both physical and behavioural signs, including the effects on communication.

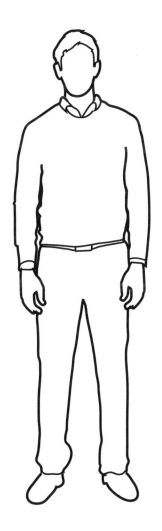

5

ii) Identify the signs that would indicate the need for specialist intervention.

_____

_____

_____

iii) Identify three sources of specialist intervention and describe how each could be accessed. Use the table below to record your answers.

Specialist intervention	How to access
1	
2	
3	

BTEC: Unit 7: 6.1, 6. 2
Diploma: Unit 7: 6.1, 6.2
PLTS: IE3, CT1, EP1, EP2, EP3

(Task 2)

Read the following case study:

Following an accident at work three months ago, James is now a wheelchair user and also has limited mobility in his right arm. He relies on domiciliary support for his daily living activities. James's life has changed considerably since his accident as he is unlikely to be able to return to his job in the leisure industry and he rarely sees his friends. Initially James was positive about his future but recently he has become isolated and feels that he has lost his self-identity. His self-esteem is poor. James's domiciliary care worker is becoming concerned about his physical and mental health and well-being.

i) Explain the links between James's self-identity and self-esteem and his well-being.

_____

_____

_____

_____

_____

ii) Describe the attitudes and approaches which his care worker should take which would help to promote his well-being.

_____

_____

_____

_____

_____

BTEC: Unit 7: 4.1, 4.2, 4.3, 4.4
Diploma: Unit 7: 4.1, 4.2
Unit 51: 1.2
PLTS: EP1, EP2, EP3, EP4, EP5, CT1, CT3, IE3

Task 3

i) Write a definition of active participation in the space below.

_____

_____

_____

ii) Produce a leaflet for new staff at your organisation.

You should include:

- a description of ways that active participation can be encouraged
- a list of barriers that may work to prevent active participation
- a description of ways that any barriers can be reduced
- a description of the benefits for the individuals
- an explanation of how active participation promotes independence in daily living.

Use the space below to plan your leaflet.

Ways to encourage participation	
Barriers	
Ways to reduce barriers	
Benefits / promotion of independent living	

5

EVIDENCE GATHERING

In this activity you will identify an area of your work that will capture evidence of how you are sensitive to the needs of individuals and can provide support at times when they are showing signs of distress.

Your assessor will help you to identify suitable items of evidence.

You need to gather evidence of activity within areas of your work to demonstrate:

Diploma: Unit 55: 2.1, 3.2, 3.3, 3.4, 4.1, 4.2, 4.3, 4.4

you can support a distressed person.

Suggested evidence may include:

a log or diary

b witness testimony

c reflective account.

BTEC: Unit 7: 6.3
Diploma: Unit 7: 4.3, 6.3, 6.4
Unit 56: 2.2
Unit 58: 5.1
PLTS: CT1, CT2, EP4

PUTTING IT INTO PRACTICE

This activity will enable your assessor to examine your competence by observing you carrying out workplace activities. Remember that you must obtain consent from the individual and your manager for this observation to take place. This might include asking related questions to test your underpinning knowledge.

Working well with an individual to help them participate actively and boost their well-being.

Your assessor will agree a time when they can observe you interacting with an individual as you support their care plan. The activity will depend upon the organisation where you work but should be part of your normal role. The assessor will observe how you encourage the person to participate in discussions about their care plan. They will also want to see that you find ways to encourage the individual to actively participate, identifying and reducing any barriers which may prevent their participation. Throughout the observation you must show that you respect the individual's sense of dignity and can promote their self-esteem. This will include how you support them to manage their personal appearance.